Sight Alignment
Trigger Control
&
The Big Lie

by
M/Sgt. JIM OWENS

JAFEICA Publishing
Enterprise, Alabama

7th Edition

ISBN 978-1-939812-67-4
(rev. b)

Also available as an ebook for:
- Kindle
- iBooks
- Nook
- Kobo

Visit our website at:
www.jarheadtop.com

Print design by
LOOSE CANNON ENTERPRISES
Paradise, CA
www.loose-cannon.com

ABOUT THE AUTHOR

In 1963, when Jim joined the Marine Corps, he had no experience with firearms. One of the Drill Instructors wore an Expert Badge, that's Jim's primary recollection of him. The EXPERT MARKSMANSHIP MEDAL hanging on his chest—and Jim wanted one just like it! Jim came home from boot camp carrying his first of many Marksmanship trophies—and wearing the gleaming silver EXPERT BADGE!

During his Marine Corps career, he acted as coach and firing member of the Marksmanship Training Unit at MCAS, Cherry Point, N.C. He's fired in the Eastern, Far Eastern, Western and Pacific Marine Corps Division Matches. (Each of these matches includes one week of classes. Thus Jim has over 500 hours of classroom training, over and above the firing line experience.)

In 1968, Jim had the opportunity to try out for the Olympic Pistol Team. The final stage of that competition is 4 SECONDS OF PURE PANIC! Jim hit two targets, a paste bucket and a score keeper. It was somewhere in that time frame that Jim realized that rifle shooting was his forte. Jim was also a Marksmanship Instructor at the U. S. Naval Academy.

He went on to become coach, as well as firing member of base teams at MCB, Camp Pendleton, CA and MCB, Quantico, VA for the Inter-service and National Matches in 1981 and 1983. In 1982 he coached the winning six man Team in the All Marine Corps Championships.

In his shooting career, he's earned 3 Bronze Legs, 1 Silver Leg, 1 Gold Leg and a Distinguished Badge. He's a High Master and a member of the 495 Club.

Since retiring as a M/SGT in 1986, Jim's been actively engaged in promoting excellence in the sport and civilian participation in Competitive High Power Shooting. He uses Racine County Line Rifle Club (WI) as his home base and experimental lab.

To ward off winter BLAH's (a.k.a. "Range's Snowed Over!"), in 1988, at the urging of Bob Schanen, Jim began holding Feb. – Apr. classes in technique, personal training, equipment handling, etc. From those humble beginnings (6 men in Bob's basement) evolved what in 1992 equaled in excess of 100 participants (men, women and juniors) in a two-phase (Basic and Advanced) training program.

This book is the result of numerous requests for more classes on Wind Reading...He had to have an "outline"!
For more information on holding Marksmanship Training classes in your area, call or write:

Jim Owens
112 Red Wing Dr.
Enterprise, AL 36330
(334) 347-0020

This book is dedicated....

To high power rifle competitive shooters everywhere. To High Power Competitive Shooters from time immemorial, who've operated under the influence of the available technology; To those same shooters, willing to embrace the change and excel in their discipline

and

To all of the shooters who've acted as my "Lab Rats".

"Challenge the Big Lie"

—Jim Owens

MEGA KUDOS TO:

Anne Wallis – whose nimble fingers on a keyboard have made this book available this year.

Jan Hickey – whose computer acumen has kept me and my machinery from self destructing.

Jon Wilcox – whose legal mind and lead pencil have kept this from being a one sentence book.

Bill Wallis – for his "Dark Room Magic"

Lee Walker of Walker Business Services – for the computer generated graphics in this book, desktop publishing, typesetting, editing and the patience of a saint.

and, to

Robbie, my wife of 40 years – for recognizing my new "Mistress", the 486DX computer, as being of no greater threat than my other "Mistresses": my Winchester Model 70, 300 Win. Mag. and Canvass Shooting Jacket.
Note: Robbie passed away in 2004

AND a big thank you to my new wife Corrie (2013) for all the help in editing this monster.

Table of Contents

CHAPTER ONE

Former National Champion, Marine Corps Warrant Officer, Michael Pietroforte, was well aware of the importance of sight alignment and trigger control when a few of his friends tried to play with his mind. Prior to 200 yd Rapid Fire practice session, they nailed his target to a couple of 2 x 4's. When they ran the target up, they walked the target down the cat walk. While he shot at it as he followed it—he cleaned it!

Second only to safety, sight alignment and trigger control are the most important factors in shooting. You may have the best position, rifle, equipment and ammo, but you will <u>not</u> shoot well if your sight alignment and trigger control are not correct.

Some people try to teach if the sights are misaligned by only one one-thousandth (1/1000) of an inch, your shot will be off by so many inches. I do not even want to know. First of all, you are dealing with a negative. The human eye can not judge one one-thousandth of an inch. One gets so wrapped around the axle with the numbers that one forgets to work on the correct things. Most articles or books on sight alignment cover the subject pretty well, but give the single importance factor only a few lines at the end. I will get your <u>attention</u> and <u>drive home</u> the point when I reach the ONE thing that causes people to reach a plateau. Until they change their technique, they will remain on that plateau. Their scores will go no higher.

I learned to shoot in Marine Corps boot camp. I remember very well because the PMI (Primary Marksmanship Instructor) stood with a foot on each side of my body while I was in the prone position. He bent over and twisted my right ear as he was explaining the importance of using the windage knob.

Another thing I remember was the acronym they taught us to remember the proper method of sight alignment and trigger control:

B.R.A.S.S.

(Breath, Relax, Aim, Slack, Squeeze)

Unfortunately, that was as far as the instruction went. They assumed that you knew what each of these words meant or how they were applied. I view B.R.A.S.S. as a good foundation to build on.

BREATHE

You have been breathing all your life and no one had to tell you how. The new shooter will put the rifle in his shoulder and notice the sights are rising and falling as he breathes, common sense tells him to hold his breath for the full string of rapid fire. When he turns blue, he finds that doesn't work either. So he holds his breath for two or three shots and takes a quick breath between shots (Not a Good Way to Learn!). When you inhale you take in oxygen and you let out carbon dioxide as you exhale. This process clears your mind and your vision. When you are ready to take the shot, take in a full breath and let it out, then take another full breath and let it out to your normal Respiratory Pause, holding your breath as you squeeze off your shot. You are trying to get the same lung pressure each and every time. You must be consistent.

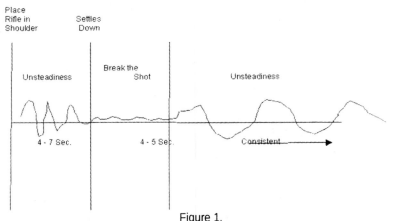

Figure 1.
A graphical description of the periods of Unsteadiness and steadiness

The amount of time you hold your breath should be no more than 10-15 seconds. (See Figure 1). When you put the rifle in your shoulder and take aim, from the point you hold your breath, your unsteadiness will be about 3-4 seconds (provided you have a good position and do all the other techniques correctly). The rifle will settle down for a period of about 4-5 seconds and with the proper sight alignment and trigger control, that is the period during which you should take the shot. Any time after that, the unsteadiness will return and it will not settle again. You must have the courage to take the rifle down and start the process over. Failure to do so will result in blurred vision, loss of mental concentration and a tendency to jerk the trigger.

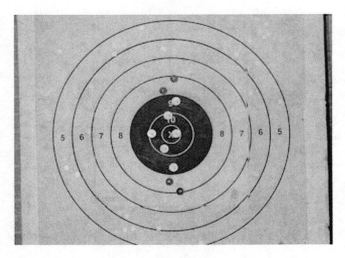

Figure 2.
A rapid fire group that is typical of improper breathing

During a string of rapid fire, **breathe between each shot**. Take in a full breath and let it out, then take in a full breath and let it out just to your respiratory pause, before holding or cutting off the breath, maintaining the same lung pressure every time. Breathing is done as you are recovering from the last shot, checking your number board and picking up your sight alignment. Do not try to hold your breath for the entire string or for more than one shot. The result of improper breathing, particularly failing to have consistent lung pressure, is shown in Figure 2. The group shown in Figure 2 can also be caused by "crawling", but that will have to wait until Chapter Ten.

RELAX

I was standing in front of my target in the pits and I overheard one shooter tell another, "You know how you tense up just before you shoot?" I gave a sideward glance and thought: "That's like saying: you know how the Sun comes up at 2:00 a.m.?" You should not tense up for a shot. You should relax and let your position take over. You will get far greater accuracy if this is done correctly.

NATURAL POINT OF AIM

Natural point of aim (also known as Natural Aiming Area or NAA in NRA books) is a subject that is often only briefly mentioned. Of course, you are told how important it is to establish your natural point of aim, but you are not told: (1) What it is; (2) How to check it; (3) How to establish it for each position; (4) How to maintain it and; (5) What does happen, when it is slightly off?

Natural point of aim is so important, it must be taught twice; once in the position classes and once in the aiming classes. <u>It must be reinforced.</u>

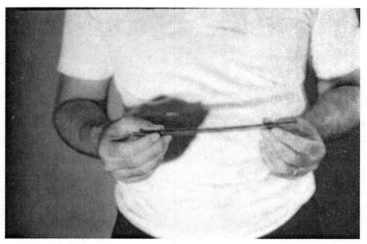

Figure 3
An Op-Rod Spring

To help get a picture of the natural point of aim, imagine a spring; an op rod spring will do. If you compress it, stretch it (a little), bend it to the right or left, up or down, you use a small amount of force. When you release the force the spring will return to its natural state or rest position. Your muscles are pretty much the same. Make a tight fist, the muscles in your forearm will be tight. You will have to hold it to keep the tight fist. If your mind wanders or you concentrate on something else (sight alignment and trigger control), your muscles want to

5

relax and return to their position, natural state.

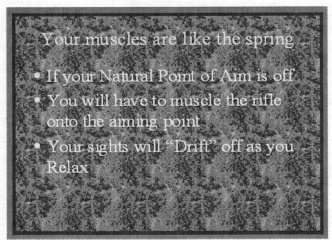

Figure 4
Your muscles are like the spring

The new shooter gets into position and puts the rifle into his shoulder and points it at his target, without regard to the natural point of aim. Remember as a kid you had the little plastic toy soldiers with the rifle in different positions; standing, kneeling and prone. When you set the toy soldier down his rifle was pointed off to the side – you had to turn him a little (his whole body) to point the rifle where you wanted it.

The new shooter sets his body down, but, since the rifle is not pointed where he wants it, he moves the rifle with his left arm to align the sights. This puts some muscle tension on the arm. His natural point of aim is where the rifle is pointed at the total rest. As he tries to perform the mechanics of shooting, his concentration is focused and his muscles relax and the spring tries to return to its natural state. Even with perfect sight alignment and trigger control, he will lose shots he should not have.

The Natural Point of Aim can be off just a little and cause you problems. Bill Wallis, the "gentleman"(?) who provides the visual aids for my high power rifle classes, was shooting off-hand at a local match. He kept putting his shots out of the ten-ring about the four o'clock position.   He looked back and wondered why.   I asked him if he had checked his natural point of aim. He did a quick check then made an adjustment – the remainder of his shots was tens and X's. He walked off the line with a sheepish look on his face!

When you set up your position during your three minute preparation period, you should establish your natural point of aim. You must first check your direction of aim.

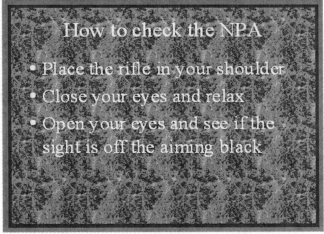

Figure 5
How to check the NPA

The first thing you do to check the natural point of aim is to put the rifle in your shoulder and get into your off-hand position.

Figure 6
Feet Placed Shoulder Width Apart

Then, close your eyes. Take two or three normal breaths. On the last breath, inhale and then exhale to your normal lung pressure, and hold while totally relaxing. Open your eyes and see if the sights are on your aiming black—do not settle for just being on your own target. The sights should be aligned <u>exactly</u> where you want them. Make minor adjustments until they do align.

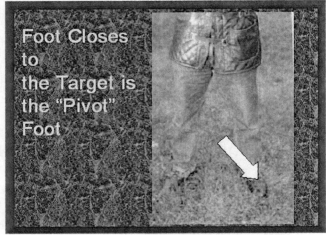

Figure 7
The Pivot Foot

8

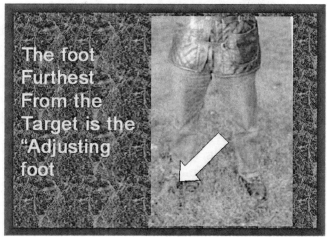

Figure 8
The Adjusting Foot

How To Adjust Your NATURAL POINT OF AIM

In the off-hand position, your feet and body are facing ninety degrees from the target and your feet are approximately shoulder width apart. To adjust your natural point of aim, move the foot that is farthest away from the target (the right foot for right-handed shooters). The left foot or the one closest to the target does not move – it is the pivot point. (See Figure 9).

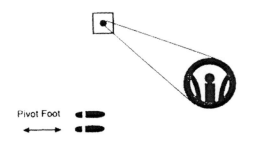

To adjust the natural point of aim, keep the left foot stationary
and move the right foot.

Figure 9
To adjust the natural point of aim, keep the left foot stationary and move the right foot.

If your natural point of aim is to the <u>left</u> of the aiming black, you need to adjust the muzzle of the rifle to the right. Simply drop the right foot back a few inches (a fraction of an inch to fine tune the position – See Figure 10). This will bring the muzzle to the right and you have adjusted your position and your natural point of aim. As you relax, your position will "float" right to the aiming black and you will not have to muscle the rifle. To correct this natural point of aim sight picture, move the right foot to the rear.

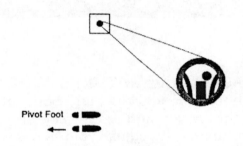

Pivot Foot

To correct this natural point of aim sight picture, move the right foot to the rear.

Figure 10
Move the Right foot back

If your position is to the <u>right</u> of the aiming black, adjust it by bringing the right foot forward. (See Figure 11) This will bring the muzzle of your rifle to the left. Again, only a fraction of an inch is needed to adjust into the correct position. You will need to check the natural point of aim after each adjustment and keep adjusting until it is correct.

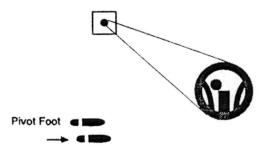

Pivot Foot

To correct this sight picture, move the right foot forward...

Figure 11
To correct this sight picture, move the right foot forward

Once you have established your natural point of aim, **YOUR FEET DO NOT MOVE!!** Moving your feet destroys the natural point of aim and you are back to square one. Every time you move your feet you set up a different natural point of aim. All of the equipment you need should be on your stool so the only movement is done by your upper body.

Adjusting the natural point of aim in the sitting position (crossed ankle) can be done by inching the right ankle forward or back to move the barrel left or right. The crossed leg and open leg positions are adjusted by moving the buttocks. The prone position is moved right or left with the hips. The up and down movement in sitting and prone position is controlled by the amount of lung pressure. Watch your front sight as you inhale, the sight will raise. As you exhale the sight will lower. Simply cut off the breath when you come to your chosen aiming point, i.e. Center Hold or Six O'clock Hold.

Keeping the feet in place in the Prone Position

Keeping the feet in place in the prone position is just as important as the off-hand position.

I was shooting a match at 1,000 yards and while keeping score for a Woman Marine Lieutenant, I noticed her feet were flopping around like a fish out of water. I told her "Keep your feet in place Lieutenant."

Here is why:

There are four elements to the aiming process. 1) the eye, 2) the rear sight, 3) the front sight and 4) the aiming black or the "Bull's Eye."

For demonstration purposes I added a fifth element. I took <u>a cleaning rod and placed it into a block of wood to hold it vertical</u>.

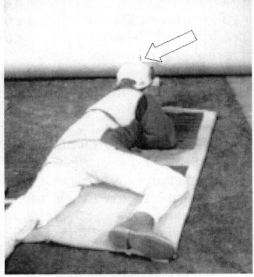

Figure 12
The arrow points to his Front Sight Post

In the picture above (Fig. 12) I placed the cleaning rod just in front of his barrel. The vertical line you see is the cleaning rod. The thick black line just above his cap is his front sight.

He now has FIVE elements in the aiming process. 1) his eye, 2) his rear sight, 3) his front sight, 4) the cleaning rod and 5) the bull's eye... all in the line of sight. He has moved his hips left or right to establish his Natural Point of Aim.

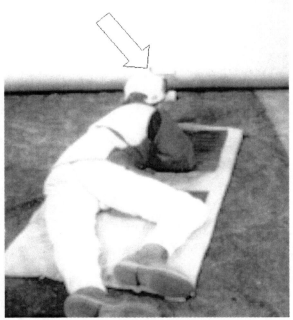

Figure 13
Feet have been moved and the Front Sight Post has moved

In the picture above (Fig. 13) I ask him to move his left foot 6-8 inches to the right. Notice the thick black spot just above his cap (His front sight) has shifted to the left of the vertical cleaning rod.

This means by moving his feet he has DESTROYED his Natural Point of Aim. If he keeps that position, he will have to use his left arm to muscle the sight back into line.

As his concentration on sight alignment, trigger control and other factors come into play his sights will drift off to his NEW Natural Point of Aim and he will lose shots and points. **KEEP YOUR FEET IN PLACE**.

CHAPTER TWO

In the mid sixties, the Cherry Point Rifle and Pistol Team shot seven days a week for nine months of the year. Weekdays were practice, and the weekends were at matches. To liven things up at one of the practice sessions, Dirty Dave Yingling (a name he worked hard acquiring) decided to play a little trick on one of his team mates.

He pasted a repair center on backwards over the aiming black of the target. He pasted an aiming black onto the metal scoring disk (a round metal disk painted red on one side and white on the other, attached to a pole about six feet long) and wrapped the pole with the white portion of the repair center.

When the targets went up for rapid fire, he held up the pole with the *mobile* aiming black in the center of the target. From the line, it looked like all of the other targets. He let the shooter pick up his sight alignment and sight picture and squeeze off the first two shots. After the magazine change and the third shot, he S-L-O-W-L-Y moved the pole around the target. Now you know why they call him Dirty Dave.

AIM

Aiming is simply aligning the front and rear sights in the proper manner. I will cover the "post" front sights first. I once had a shooter ask a question on the subject and I told him: "that was covered in the class. Weren't you paying attention?" He said: "You were talking about the M1A and I shoot an AR-15." "No—I was talking about the POST FRONT SIGHT; the method is the same for each."

Aiming involves three elements
       1. Sight Alignment
       2. Sight Picture
       3. Focus

SIGHT ALIGNMENT

The rear sight is an aperture or a small hole through a piece of metal – or a hooded rear sight. When you get into position, make sure the eye relief is the same each and every time. Eye relief is the distance from the rear sight to your eye. It is controlled by the placement of your cheek on the same spot of the stock, known as "stock weld", or the placement of your cheek onto your hand (usually the thumb), known as "spot weld". Make sure you are looking through the center of the rear sight..

When you look through the rear aperture, your mind must form an imaginary pair of cross hairs, one vertical and one horizontal. The front sight post is then aligned with these cross hairs. The top of the front sight post is brought up even with the horizontal line and centered. There is an equal amount of the front sight post on each side of the vertical line (See Figure 14).

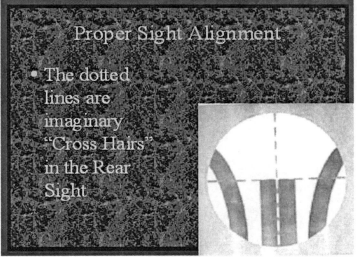

Proper Sight Alignment

- The Circle is the Rear Sight
- The Post is the Front Sight
- The curved lines are the "Wings" to protect the front sight

Figure 14
Proper Sight Alignment

Proper Sight Alignment

- The dotted lines are imaginary "Cross Hairs" in the Rear Sight

Figure 14a
Proper Sight Alignment

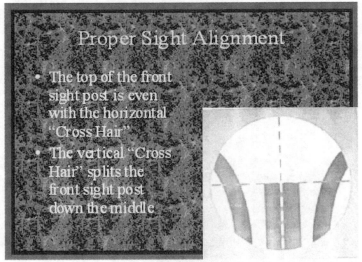

Figure 14b
Proper Sight Alignment

You cannot assume the shooter automatically knows this. We once had a shooter hitting way over the target. He was putting the BOTTOM of the front sight post even with the horizontal line.

Figure 15
Calling the Shot

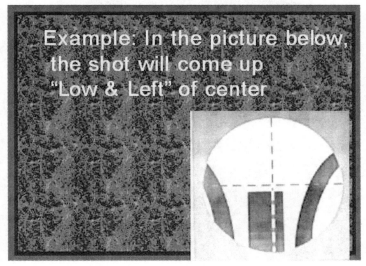

Figure 16
Sight Mis-alignment

Figure 16 is an exaggeration of sight mis-alignment. The shot will be out of the black. It will be low and to the left, and most likely off the target at longer distances. A small mis-alignment can cause you problems, but don't "get wrapped around the axle" with the thousandths of an inch—just do it correctly. It must be done the same each and every time.

SIGHT PICTURE

When you are trying to shoot at and hit an aiming point you must add the next step – "sight picture". In High Power shooting, the aiming point is a round circle, a different size for each distance. But the size of the aiming black will appear the same in the rear sight at all distances.

The most common sight picture used is the "six o'clock hold". The sight alignment is correct and the aiming black is set on top of the front sight post so the post just touches the six o'clock position of the aiming black. The sights are adjusted for the bullet to hit the center of the target. (See Figure 17). This gives the shooter a defined aiming point. For an experienced shooter, it is the best. For a new shooter, it causes a problem that will be discussed in the section on FOCUS.

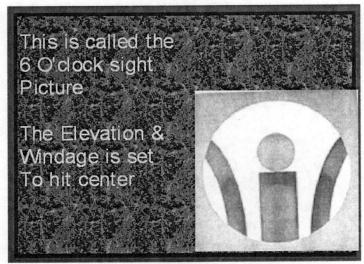

Figure 17
The 6 O'clock Hold

The "Center" or "Navy" hold is shown in Figure 18. It is also called "The Point of Aim, Point of Impact." The sight alignment is the same and the top of the front sight post is placed in the "Center of Mass" of the aiming black. The sights are adjusted so the strike of the bullet is set to "Point of Aim, Point of Impact".

Figure 18 The Center or Navy Hold

Figure 19
The Sub-Six Hold

I knew of a "Sub-Six Hold", but never used it until a particular weekend. We were shooting the Marine Corps Western Division Matches. After one week of school and three weeks of practice, getting ready for one week of matches, I was ready for a break. The local club was having a rifle match that weekend and the Major said, "You <u>will</u> shoot and you <u>will</u> have fun."

Every time I fired a Division Match, I checked out two M-14's, one as a back up gun in case something went wrong with the number one gun. This weekend both rifles were in for repairs so I drew a third rifle from the Armory and with no zero, went to shoot the match on Saturday morning. While zeroing the rifle from two hundred yards in the off-hand position (you can do things like that when you are a little show off), my first sighter was extremely high. I ran the sights all the way down to the bottom and took the second sighter. Again it was way too high, but still within the scoring rings.

In the old days, you were allowed only two sighters at each **yard line** (two sighters at the 200 yard line for both off-hand and 200 yard rapid). Since then, a new rule change allows two sighters at each **stage** (two for off-hand and two for 200 rapid

21

fire). I decided to use the sub-six hold, shoot the twenty shots off-hand, have the armorer put on a new sight, and re-zero for the sitting rapid stage.

Using proper sight alignment, I used the bottom edge of the 4'x6' target as the aiming point and had the sights set to hit the center. To my amazement, I found I could call my shots. I could tell if the shot was going to be just out of the ten ring at three o'clock.

For a period of time, I experimented with the sub-six hold (not <u>that</u> much of a sub-six hold). I held about halfway from the bottom of the black to the bottom of the target and had the sights set to hit center, while maintaining proper sight alignment (See Figure 14). I found the sub-six hold allowed me to "accept my wobble area" and continue the squeeze of the trigger without trying to make the shot "too" perfect as in the six o'clock hold. A slight call to the right still gave me a ten at three o'clock and a slight call high still gave me a ten at the 12 o'clock. The center hold works much the same

Jack Krieger, an excellent Long Range shooter and well-known rifle barrel maker, holds the world's record for a sub-six hold. We were shooting a 1,000-yard match and he brought a different rifle on the second day, but forgot to bring his sights. After asking around, he found an extra set that would fit his rifle. He took his first sighter and I saw it go half way up the side of the mountain (all right, large hill). He came all the way down to zero on the sights and still was way over the target at 1,000 yards. I had him hold on a trash can at the 600-yard line and shoot again and he was still over the target. He then held on a clump of dirt on the 800-yard line and his shot was low and left. I brought him up and right and we got onto paper...he fired a 193 with a sight picture 800 yards sub-six.

Some people use a "Line of White" hold or a "Flat Tire" hold. In the "Line of White" hold you hold just a little under the six o'clock position so there is a line of white between your front sight post and the aiming black. The "Flat Tire" hold has you pushing your front sight post up into the aiming black a little so the round aiming black appears to have a "flat tire". The problem with each of these is "How much?" and keeping each shot consistent. This is very difficult especially on a HOT day with any kind of mirage.

A "Frame" hold is used in very poor light or foggy conditions. You can barely make out the target so you shoot for the center of the frame, because the frame is all you can see.

All these sight pictures work. I have used each from time to time and I've changed around. I have practiced for weeks with the sub-six hold and the morning of the match decided to go with a center hold because it felt right.

ATTENTION!
ATTENTION!!
ATTENTION!!!

Put the book down and go take a break! Come back later when you are refreshed and can give the next section your full attention. It is so <u>important</u>; it will dramatically increase your scores and/or classification.

FOCUS

I read an article on sight alignment, and it was pretty good, but I waited to see what they had to say about the focus. Near the end of the four or five page article was one small paragraph where they stated, "The proper focus is on the front sight post not on the aiming black." That is true as far as it goes. When I started shooting High Power in 1965, I was told the same thing, but how important the focus is was not driven home.

When I started shooting, I was pretty good in the off-hand position. My rapid fire strings were OK, but my 600 yard scores were terrible. I had elevation problems you wouldn't believe. I tried *everything*, six o'clock hold, center hold, subsix hold, and line of white hold, flat tire hold, and frame hold. I held the bottom of the target. I held the top of the berm and nothing helped. I could not hold elevation well enough to keep the shots in the black, much less the ten ring. <u>I changed one thing</u> – <u>my focus!!</u> My elevation at 600 yards dropped to the X-ring size and I went from getting bronze medals to silver and gold medals. My scores and classification shot up. I am now a "reformed non-focuser" and will talk to anyone who will listen.

During my advance class in High Power (And in Chapter Ten of this book), I show a series of color slides, about 15 of them on rapid fire groups. Each group is different and there is a reason the group is the way it is. I show each slide twice. The first time I put the slide up for about 15-20 seconds without saying anything. The students look at each group and try to recognize his or her groups. The second time, we talk about what causes the group, and how to correct it.

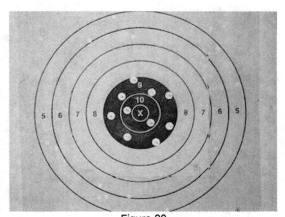

Figure 20
A typical group caused by improper focus.

The first time I ran this part of the class, I was running through the first set. When we came to the slide that looks like Figure 20, about 75% of the faces in the audience lit up. I said, "Oh, you recognize your group." The second time I gave that class, we had close to 100 people, and again, about 75% of the faces lit up.

The cause of having a group like that is, first, <u>improper focus.</u> There is a second reason and I will cover it in that section.

AN EXPERIMENT

With the sun or a strong light behind and above your shoulders, put your right hand at arm's length and down at a 45 degree angle with your index finger extended and the finger print facing you. Place your left elbow against your side and place your left hand in front of your body. (This gives the proper distance between fingers). Again extend the index finger with the prints facing you. Make sure the finger on your left hand does not block the view of the finger on the right hand. The two fingers should be close together in the line of sight, positioned so you can see both at the same time. The fingers should be 10-12 inches apart.

Figure 21
Focusing on the Finger Prints

Focus your vision on the finger closest to you until you can see the finger <u>prints</u>. You can still see the other finger, but you *cannot* see the prints. Shift your focus to the finger on the right hand and focus on the prints; you can still see the other finger, but you cannot see the prints. THE HUMAN EYE CANNOT FOCUS ON TWO OBJECTS AT DIFFERENT DISTANCES AT THE SAME TIME!!!

You can rapidly shift your focus from one finger to the other and convince yourself you are focusing on both—YOU ARE NOT.

Another example, as you are watching a movie or TV program, the camera is focused on the person standing closest to it and the image is sharp and clear. The person standing in the distance (3 or 4 feet away) is blurred – you can see them but they are not clear. The cameraman changes the focus as the other person starts to speak, that person becomes clear and you see the one nearest the camera start to go out of focus. Because of the distance, the camera, like the human eye, cannot focus on two objects at the same time. They can be *seen* but not focused.

Let's apply this to shooting

In the aiming process, we start with your eye. I have already covered eye relief, keeping the eye the same distance from the rear sight each time. The ideal situation calls for your head to be erect and you looking straight through the rear sight, but, due to the different positions, this is not always possible. Your head may be down and you are looking through the top portion of your glasses.

Most people recommend you shoot with both eyes open. They say closing the left eye puts a strain on the right eye. After awhile, you get a slight quiver in the muscles around the eye. I tried shooting with both eyes open and did just as well as with one eye closed. It felt so strange that it bothered me. (Forty year habits are hard to break).

The line of sight goes from the eye, through the rear sight aperture (the mind forms the imaginary cross hairs). The front sight post is then brought into the line of sight and correctly aligned with the imaginary cross hairs. By placing the aiming black in the final stages of the process, and forming the sight picture, you have the process taught to most people.

Little or no attention is given to the proper focus. The front sight post is the proper place to focus and is critical to good shooting and scores. Picture the front sight post as the finger closest to you and the aiming black

As the finger furthest away. Even if it is 200 yards, 300 yards or 600 yards, you must **always** focus on the **front sight post**!!

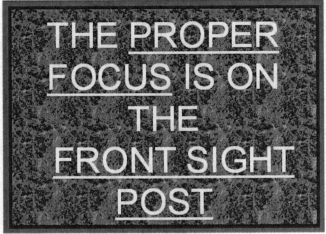

Figure 22
Proper Focus

Remember I said I had trouble holding the elevation at 600 yards. Well, after someone told me about the finger print experiment I tried something. (I'll skip the hard way I took at the time). This piece marked in red is the old information, **DO NOT** take a number two pencil and draw a diagonal line on your front post. (See Figure 28). This acts as the finger prints, and when in focus, <u>will not</u> allow you to focus on the target.

STOP

Again, DO NOT take a number two pencil and draw a diagonal line on your front post. That was in the original book, a much better way is shown below.

NOTE

Take a look at the paragraph above. I said "I'll skip the hard way I took at the time." Well, sometimes reality yanks my choker chain. As it turned out "the hard way" worked a lot better. So my advice is to skip "the number two pencil mark" and go with the hard way. It worked for me and I now use it in all my classes. Here is what I have them do.

First we must define our terms. The front sight post, I am

talking about the part that is closest to the shooter, in other words, the part that FACES the shooters eye. Not the sides, top or far side. Just the part of the post that you see when looking through the rear sight.

The first thing I do is have the students clean the front sight post (Carbon, dust dirt etc).

Next they take a Q-tip and break it in half. Then use the stem, (not the cotton swab) and dip the stem into yellow model airplane paint.

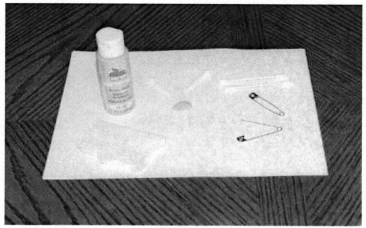

Figure 23
Supplies

With the rifle upside down, the muzzle resting on a data book (to protect the crown) place the stem of the Q-tip with paint onto the front sight post. **The Crown and it's importance to the accuracy of your rifle is explained in Chapter Six.**

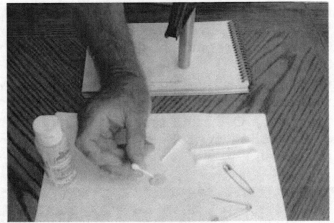
Figure 24
Dip the Stem into the Paint

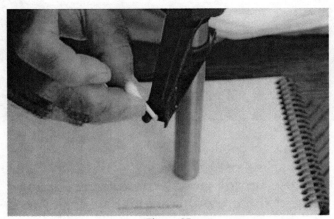
Figure 25
Place the paint onto the Front Sight Blade

Figure 26
Let the Paint Dry

Give the paint a few minutes to dry.

Figure 27
Make a scratch in the paint

Then using a safety pin, draw a scratch in the paint **from lower left to upper right**.

Figure 28
The scratch in the paint now acts as a fingerprint

The scratch in the paint now acts as a fingerprint. If you are focused on this scratch, you CANNOT be focused on the target. The target will be out of focus but you can still see it and your point of aim.

Once I started focusing on my front sight post, I also went to a "center hold". My elevation problems at 600 yards were reduced to X-ring elevation spread.

I put the post into the aiming black and let my position take over. I did not try to get it absolutely perfect. You close the bolt, put the rifle into your shoulder, check your number board, take your breath as you put the front sight post into the black, and focus on the scratch in the paint as you squeeze off the shot.

My elevation problems reduced tremendously. In fact, they came down to almost X-ring size (I had a student in Las Vegas who had the same results.) I now could pay more attention to the wind. I thought, "If this works at 600 yards, it should work at 300." It did. How about 200 yards – surprise again, it worked.

We fired a match at Twenty Nine Palms, CA. My first ten shots off-hand was all in the black. I had two tens and eight shots were nines. I realized I had been focusing on the target.

I even remember seeing the orange scoring disk. After I gave myself a mental drop kick, I fired the second ten shots, <u>this time focusing on the front sight post.</u> They were all in the black, eight tens and Xs and two nines. Changing the focus brought in the wide shots. From that day on I have been like a reformed alcoholic. I preach focusing to anyone who will listen. Shooting leg matches, up to that time, I had three bronze medals. After I started focusing, I got a silver and a gold medal, to go Distinguished.

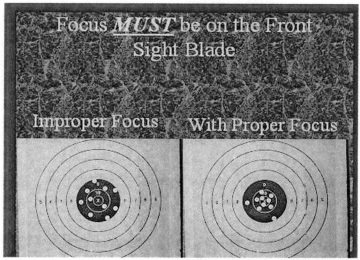

Figure 29
Focus MUST be on the Front Sight Blade

You can tell if your focus is correct by your "call". Calling predicts where the shot will be on the target, based on how your sight alignment and sight picture looked. If you called it a ten at six and it is a ten at six, then you are <u>on call</u>. If you called it a ten at six and it is a ten at twelve, then you are off call and you should adjust your sights. A young lady on the Marine Corps Team last year said it very well, "If your shot is <u>within</u> your call, your focus is correct, if it is <u>outside</u> your call, your focus is incorrect."

Is It Legal?

I first started using the yellow paint on my front sight post during the Marine Corps Eastern Division leg Matches in 1967. I had a small problem with my M-14 rifle and I took it over to the armors van.

The armorer, a Marine Corps Staff/Sgt. said in a very nasty tone of voice "That's not legal." I asked "What?" He said "The paint on the front sight." I asked "Why?" He made up a term out of thin air "External Modification." I replied "So is blackening your sights, @$*#"

A few years later I talked to the head referee at Camp Perry during the National Rifle Matches and he said "There is nothing illegal about using the paint on the front sight post."

Problems With the Six O'clock Hold

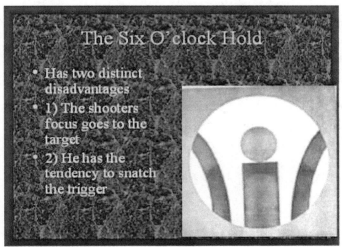

Figure 30
Two Disadvantages

For an experienced shooter, the 6 o'clock hold is great. However, I feel (for a new shooter) the 6 o'clock hold has two distinct disadvantages. The 6 o'clock hold gives a person a "defined" aiming point – 6 o'clock. The trouble is a thing called "wobble area." The rifle in the offhand position "wobbles" around the black. I for example, have the wobble area the size of Cleveland.

The new shooter tries to break the shot when the sights touch the 6 o'clock position of the bulls-eye. As a result he "snatches" the trigger ("Get it NOW"), resulting in poor trigger control and some very wide shots.

The second disadvantage for the new shooter is improper focus. The shooter tends to focus on the bull's-eye, but it belongs on the front sight post.

When the front sight is below the bulls-eye and down in the white area, the shooter can focus on the mark on the front sight post and can apply the correct trigger control.

One time in the classroom, an Air Force Reserve Col. said "Jim, are you telling these people to NOT USE THE 6 O'CLOCK

35

HOLD?" I thought for a second and replied "YES."

One time on the firing line, while the students were trying the Sub-6 o'clock hold, a Navy lieutenant Commander was shooting his offhand. He had never shot a Sub-6 o'clock hold before. One of his troops was calling the shots for him. His man was calling 10,10,X,10,X,10, 9,10,X,10. The lieutenant Commander thought his man was screwing with him. When they walked down range, he had a score of 99 -3Xs. It was the best score he had ever fired.

Another time a shooter looked back at me and said "This is voodoo." and I told them "Yes, but it works."

CHAPTER THREE

I always thought that when I got to be elderly that becoming a "dirty old man" was going to be fun. No one told me that you lose your eye sight and hearing, your body aches all over, and you get ugly. Oh well, I saw a sign that says, "Old age ain't for wimps."

APERTURE SIGHTS

I learned to shoot aperture sights long before my eyes started to go and I'm glad I did. I will admit that it helps tremendously to be young and have good eyes to shoot a "post" front sight. Aperture sights, sometimes called "globe" front sights, are far easier on the eyes. There is no need for the constant focus.

With the aperture, sight alignment and sight picture are the same. You have three concentric circles. The rear sight, front sight and the aiming black <u>must</u> all have the same center.

Figure 31   Three Concentric Circles

The front sight is an aperture, or circle, and it must have the center aligned with the rear sight. Place the aiming black into the front aperture and its center must be concentric with the others. **Have an equal amount of white around the aiming black ensures that it is centered**.

When you look through the rear sight, make sure you have the same "eye relief" each and every time. Once again, eye relief is the distance from the rear sight to your eye. It is controlled by the placement of your cheek on the same spot of the stock, known as "stock weld", or the placement of your cheek onto your hand (usually the thumb), known as "spot weld". Make sure you are looking through the center of the rear sight.

Everything I have told you to this point is true—as far as it goes. That was all that I was taught, and I made the same mistakes most new shooters make. I started to learn what works and what doesn't.

THE FRONT APERTURE
(Logic Takes a Holiday)

When I started to shoot a Match Rifle with aperture sights I was told about the three concentric circles and told to line them up with the same center and to make sure the aiming black was centered in the front aperture with an equal amount of white all around it. That was all I was told.

Figure 32

Like 98% of the other new shooters, I made the same mistake. My front aperture looked like Figure 33. I had too tight a line of white around the aiming black. Logic said that it would be easier to judge if it was centered and I could pick up small misalignment of the sights.

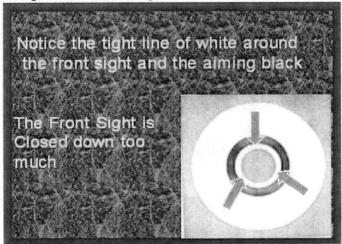

Notice the tight line of white around the front sight and the aiming black

The Front Sight is Closed down too much

Figure 33
A common error with new shooters is to make the front aperture very small.

Too tight a line of white actually makes it <u>harder</u> for your eyes to distinguish when you are lined up. It causes eyestrain, fatigue and creates undue tension as you shoot. It can create fuzziness and distort the image as you try to break the shot.

By experimenting, I gradually opened the front aperture and, gradually, I shot better. I read several articles which said the front aperture should be <u>two or two and a half</u> times the size of the aiming black (See Figure 34). I was amazed because my previous logic told me otherwise, but since I was improving by opening the aperture a little, I tried the suggested larger opening. My scores got even better.

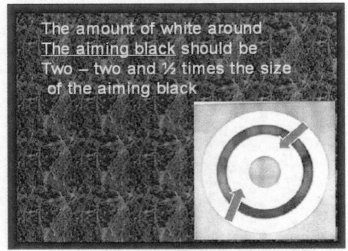

The amount of white around
The aiming black should be
Two – two and ½ times the size
of the aiming black

Figure 34
A front aperture that is bigger, greatly improves accuracy.

The front aperture should be 2 OR 2-1/2 times the size of the aiming black

Someone asked "how do I tell if I have the 2 - 2 1/2 times ratio to the aiming black?"

The simple way is to have the rifle pointed at the target, either while in the prone position or having a rifle laying on the shooting stool. Center the aiming black in the center of the front aperture front sight. The bull's-eye will not move, so gently push the front of the rifle to the right. Stop pushing when the 9 o'clock position of the bulls-eye touches the inside of the front aperture.

Now draw an imaginary vertical crosshair down the center of the front aperture. If the crosshair touches the bull's-eye at the 3 o'clock position, your front aperture is open far enough for twice the size of the aiming black. In other words you have one to the left of the line and you could fit another one to the right of the line. See Fig. 35

Having the front aperture open even a little further, so the crosshair is off to the right side of the 3 o'clock position of the bull gives you a little more than twice the ratio.

Figure 35
The front aperture should be 2 OR 2-1/2 times the size of the aiming black

Someone asked "how do I tell if I have the 2 – 2 1/2 times ratio to the aiming black?"

The simple way is to have the rifle pointed at the target, either while in the prone position or having a rifle laying on the shooting stool. Center the aiming black in the center of the front aperture front sight. The bull's-eye will not move, so gently push the front of the rifle to the right. Stop pushing when the 9 o'clock position of the bulls-eye touches the inside of the front aperture.

Now draw an imaginary vertical crosshair down the center of the front aperture. If the crosshair touches the bull's-eye at the 3 o'clock position, your front aperture is open far enough for twice the size of the aiming black. In other words you have one to the left of the line and you could fit another one to the right of the line. See Fig. 35

Having the front aperture open even a little further, so the crosshair is off to the right side of the 3 o'clock position of the bull gives you a little more than twice the ratio.

It may seem a little strange, but stick with it and the results will show in the improved scores. Don't try to make your sight picture too good. The aiming black self centers as you fire your rapid fire. I tried to make it "Just Right", and it messed up my timing. In one of the "STAR WARS" movies, Luke

41

Skywalker was learning to use the light saber – he was told something like, "Don't use your eyes, just 'feel' it, let it happen." Don't try to make it too good; just feel it and let it happen. You will be surprised at how much better you shoot and you can call your shots far better.

During the slow fire, you want to make each shot just right. Your eyes will automatically center the aiming black but you are not sure, "Is it centered?" You take it off-center just a little and say, "Yep, that was centered", and you then re-center it. After a while, you will know exactly when it is centered. Quite often, just as it is centered up, the image will "brighten" just a little. For me, it is like a one-watt light bulb was turned on and I know it's time to break the shot.

Do not "lie" on the rifle and take an extra long time trying to make the shot perfect. Once you close the bolt, check the wind, and make an adjustment if needed., then place the rifle in your shoulder, roll into it, take your breath as you are checking your number board, pick up your sight alignment and squeeze off the shot. You should complete the process in about one half the time it takes to read this paragraph. If you stare at the sight picture, the sights will be "burned" into your mind and you can misalign the sights, still thinking they are correct. 3-5 seconds—no more.

Figure 36

THE MOST COMMON MISTAKES MADE BY NEW SHOOTERS

For the most part, High Power Shooters are great people and are willing to help. Remember, on the firing line, the seasoned shooter is trying to get ready for the same match you are. He may be getting mentally prepared and if you ask a lot of questions, it may be irritating. After the match, you cannot go up and say, "Tell me everything you know". That could take awhile. You have to know what questions to ask.

After much "trial and error", I found the correct method and amount of adjustment for both the front and rear sights. One day, I knew the right questions and who to ask. Col. Sam Burkhalter has been the Senior National Champion more times than he cares to admit, and when it comes to helping other shooters, he is a gymnast of the first order. He will bend over backwards to help.

During one conversation, Sam said, "That's right! Most new shooters have the front aperture closed down to far, and the rear aperture opened up too far."

THE REAR SIGHT

During your prep time, while looking through the sight, close down the **rear** sight aperture <u>all</u> the way down, then <u>slowly</u> open it to the point where a flood of light comes in and your eye relaxes. <u>STOP</u> at that point. DO NOT open it any further. This is not a case of "if a little is good, a lot is better." Opening it further will be much like the improper focus with the post front sight. You will get wide shots – nines when they should be ten's or Xs.

Let's talk about the Match Rifle rear sight. Today's technology makes the sight almost a work of art and you can get one with all the "bells and whistles" like I did. I have both the *Warner and **Zelenak sights and they both are excellent sights – both come in ¼ or 1/8 minute clicks and both require the aperture to be purchased separately. * Warner Tool Company 603-352-9521 ** Zelenak it would seem is no longer in business.

The Gehmann aperture is a fine choice. Here is where all the "bells and whistles" come in...but also the trouble! The features available are: **adjustable iris** (The hole or aperture you look thru opens and closes.), **polarizing filters**, **five colored filters** and a **diopter**. The adjustable iris is a <u>must</u>; it is the part that opens and closes to let in more or less light. This is the one most new shooters open to far. The ability to open or close the rear aperture is one of the match sights' strong points and you <u>do</u> want it.

The sight comes with two polarizing filters, which are nothing more than a lens with finely etched lines very close together. As you drop the filter down into the line of sight, it refines or filters to one plane of light, and gives the aiming black a sharp, clear contrast against the background. It's mostly used on a bright day and it will cut the glare. I only use one of the two filters because using both just makes it too dark. When I first got the sight, I thought there would be instructions on how to use the polarizing filters. There were instructions, but they were in German and with a lot of effort I had them translated – it was how to break the filters down for cleaning, not how to use them. Using only one polarizing filter works fine for me. It is a nice feature and you will like it.

SAVE YOUR MONEY

Unless you are among the one or two percent of shooters who use a lot of colored glasses in different light conditions, save your money and don't get the aperture with the five colored filters. You'll find you just don't use them.

I didn't know what a diopter was until I saw one at Camp Perry. A diopter is a magnifier, either on the front or rear sight. You may not use both. It is said to act as a telescope and is not legal. (More on the front diopter later).

When I first got the Gehmann aperture with the rear diopter, the salesman said: "Hold it up and look through it at a distant object and turn the ring." It was like a miniature spotting scope. You could bring the distant object into focus, just like a scope. You could see the aiming black clearer, sharper and bigger (closer). You can use it at all ranges from 200 yards to 1,000 yards. "Oh boy, I've got to have this."

I bought the rear diopter at Camp Perry in August and used it up until the beginning of October, with no problems. When we started shooting in April, I was having one hell of a time shooting. My shots would go wide at nine o'clock and I would come right. It would be all right for a while, but then I would get another wild shot out the left and again come right. It kept doing that for sometime. Someone said, "It's early in the season. Everyone has problems. You'll settle in." For three matches, my scores went from High Master down to expert. I was ready to sell a $500 sight for $75. Luckily, Rocky, one of the shooters on the line, didn't take me up on the offer.

I gave the sight to Boots Obermeyer to check out. He put it on a dial indicator and found it was tracking perfectly. "It might be the diopter," he said. I told him, "I know how to find out." On the next Wednesday night practice, I put up a 600 yard reduced target at 200 yards and from the prone position; I fired my first ten shots – the same problem continued. I got out of position and removed the aperture with the diopter and replaced it with a plain aperture with just an adjustable iris, *no* diopter. I lay back down and fired the second ten shots and got a 99 with 6 Xs. I talked to the salesman at Camp Perry that year, and he said, "The rear diopter was made for Small Bore shooting and High Power shooters discovered them, but they are not designed for the punishment and shock High Power gives them."

Save your money – stay away from the rear diopter. By dropping from High Master to Expert, I knew something was wrong. A Marksman or a Sharpshooter may think, "It must be me" and he will continue to shoot with bad equipment. Your RIFLE, SIGHTS, AMMO and EQUIPMENT must be better than you are. If any one of these is a limiting factor, you will shoot up to "it's" ability and not "yours."

NOTE: All of the above applies to "Match Rifles" (Bolt Guns and Semi-auto match rifles, commonly called "Space Guns") However, SERVICE RIFLES (Ar-15s, M1As and the M-1 Garand) that have a "Hooded" rear sight may have a diopter in the rear sight and they are legal for both NRA & CMP matches.

THE FRONT SIGHTS

I used the "Drop In" apertures, both metal and plastic. They are all right, but use an adjustable one once and you'll never go back to the drop in type. I tend to use one setting for all yard lines on a given day. I use the same setting for off-hand, 200 yard rapid, 300 yard rapid and 600 yard prone as long as I keep the 2-2 1/2 ratio of white around the aiming black. The light conditions for this weekend may not allow the use of the same setting you used last weekend. You may not even think about it until you look down range through the sights at the start of your three minute prep time. After using the full three minutes to get the right drop in aperture, I decided to switch to an adjustable one. You reach up and dial it like a radio and it takes just seconds.

I'm using a Gehmann adjustable aperture on an Anschutz base, with an Eagle Eye Diopter.

THE FRONT DIOPTER

If you have ever fired the 1,000 yard iron sight matches at Camp Perry you know they import fog and/or haze just for that match. Finding your own number board twenty times in a row is a major accomplishment.

I have this little demonstration I do when explaining a front diopter. I do it at the 200 yard line, but it will work at any yard line. I first take the diopter out (it just unscrews) and I have the person look through the sights at the aiming black just the way it would normally appear. I then screw the diopter back in and I have them look again. You should see their faces light up. One shooter said, "I've got to get one of these."

The .3 diopter can be used at the 200 yard, 300 yard and 600 yard lines. I leave it in for shooting across the course. Make sure you take it out and clean it before each day of shooting. It makes the image so much sharper, clearer and larger. You must see it to believe it. The .3 diopter can

Also be used for the 800 yard, 900 yard and 1,000 yard lines. You can see your number board and the aiming black.

The .5 diopter is best used at 900 yards and 1,000 yards. It is very strong. Shooting 1,000 yards with a .5 diopter makes it appear as if the aiming black is at only 600 yards. You can shoot so much better when you can see.

I tried the .5 diopter at 600 yards to see what would happen. I fired the first ten shots with it and it really brought the aiming black in close. I was getting some pretty wide shots, so, after the ten shots, I took the .5 diopter out and put in the .3 diopter. I immediately knew what the problem was. The .5 magnified it so much, it looked like Figure 33 and there was too tight of a line of white around the aiming black. The .3 made it look like Figure 32, with the correct amount of white, 2-2 ½ times. The second ten shots were all tens and Xs – no more wide shots.

The adjustable, front diopter magnifies everything. If you are using the Gehmann adjustable you have to open it even farther than normal. I was using the model that opened to 4.2 and I had it opened all the way. This didn't leave any room for bad light conditions. Last year at Camp Perry, I sold it and I got the newer model that opens to 4.8. Everyone I know that has used the front diopter has liked it. My recommendation for High Power: "Stay away from the rear diopter. It may never give you trouble, but if it does it will be BIG trouble."

CHAPTER FOUR

SLACK

The M-14 has a two-stage trigger. The first stage has what is called "slack"; you pull the trigger through the slack until you feel it stop. The second stage requires a force of at least four and one half pounds to make the hammer fall and fire the rifle. I thought that was pretty simple and straightforward and I couldn't mess it up. I WAS WRONG!!! We went to the range on New Years Day and I did a little shooting. While I was in the pits, pulling my target, one of the shooters who had attended my High Power Rifle Class said he thought what I meant by "slack" was to put the rifle in your shoulder and, with a good grip, pull the stock back into your shoulder, taking up the slack. I swear, some days I can ruin an anvil with a rubber mallet.

SQUEEZE

Squeeze is nothing more than applying firm pressure to the trigger – straight to the rear without disturbing the sights. Easier said than done. Right? Well there are some other things to add that will help you do this. There are two basic methods: (1) the uninterrupted and (2) the interrupted method.

Using the **interrupted** method you start the trigger squeeze and maintain your sight alignment. As the sights drift off the "sight picture" or your "aiming point" (i.e., six o'clock hold), you <u>stop</u> the trigger squeeze but you <u>do not</u> let off the pressure. You hold the pressure at that point, interrupting the trigger squeeze. As the sights come back to the point of aim, you continue the squeeze. Most often used in the Off Hand or Standing Position.

The **Uninterrupted** is applying pressure to the trigger—straight to the rear without disturbing the sights and without stopping. Commonly used in all long range and rapid fire strings.

Figure 20 in Chapter Two, shows the shots scattered in no particular pattern. The main cause was improper focus. Another cause is poor trigger control, especially in the off-hand position (See Figure 37). The shots are further from the center than you would have with improper focus. OK, fine, but how do we get the proper trigger control? First, we have to learn the mechanics and the things to do and/or not to do. We then have to work on it: a lot of dry firing. We have to do some exercises to the point it becomes automatic; second nature; autopilot. You do it without thinking. If something goes wrong, your finger must instantly come off the trigger.

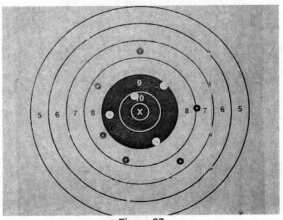

Figure 37
A typical group fired by a shooter having poor trigger control,
particularly evident in the off-hand position.

The instructions here will be for the off-hand position. There is a little more involved here than the other positions. The instructions for off-hand position will cover all the others. The first thing to do is take a look at your hand. Examine the palm. From the center of the palm up to the base of the thumb is a meaty part that looks like a drumstick on a chicken leg, especially if you move the thumb slightly towards the little finger.

While we are doing the examination of the hand, bend the trigger finger toward you so you can see the finger nail. Look at the tip of the finger, and then look at the back of the fingernail, the part that is known as the "quick". Now turn the finger over and look at the pad of flesh directly opposite the quick. <u>This</u> is the part of the finger that should touch the trigger. Not the finger tip and no further back than the first joint.

Now look at the second joint. When you grip the rifle at the small of the stock and place your finger on the trigger, make sure the back part of the finger near the second joint does not lie tightly onto the stock (called "Dragging Wood").

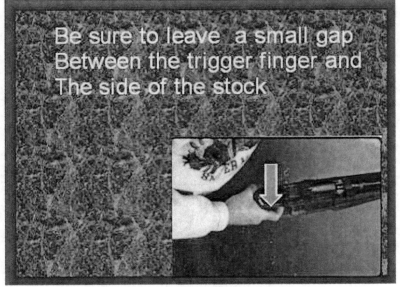

Figure 38

This would prevent you from pulling the trigger straight to the rear. You would push it to the side, taking the front sight with it. Your group would look like Figure 39.

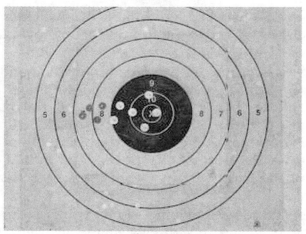

Figure 39
A group that is typical of a shooter who is "dragging wood".

Now that we have some individual pieces of this puzzle, let's put them together. When you get ready to shoot off-hand or any other position, consistency is important. You must do it the same every time. When you close the bolt (in a safe direction – down range), you start by placing your hand on the small of the stock. Look at the "drumstick" meaty part of the palm and make sure it comes in contact with the same part of the stock each and every time, usually just to the right of the centerline.

Now wrap your hand around the small of the stock and get a good grip. The trigger finger is placed on the trigger, in the manner described above, making sure you are not "dragging wood". The three lower fingers come on around the small of the stock and meet the thumb on the grip.

The grip should be like a good <u>firm</u> handshake. If you put on a "death grip", you will have muscle tension and it will shake. If the grip is too loose (Sgt. Roxburgh used to call it a "Fifi grip"), you will not have control, and a 4 ½ pound trigger pull will feel like ten pounds.

There are several exercises you can do at home. Just make sure the rifle is safe—unloaded. Wives or girlfriends get <u>very</u> upset with bullet holes in the ceiling. The first exercise you can do while sitting on the couch in the living room or just about anywhere. With the magazine out and the rifle clear, close the bolt and get a grip as explained above. With your eyes closed, <u>feel</u> the trigger pull as you squeeze the trigger.

Try to take up about one half of the trigger pressure and hold it, and then take up the other half of the pressure until the hammer falls. Repeat this again and again. Some people find they can do it right away while others have to work harder at it. It may require dozens of times or hundreds of times, but do it until it becomes second nature. It will help your off-hand scores tremendously.

At the State Service Rifle Championship, they gave a special award to the "High Marine," active or former. One of my students won it and he wrote a letter to me.

"Jim, I tried your exercise on taking up one half the trigger pull and holding it. I practiced for one hour each night for the months of April, May and June. My scores went up from the 450's to the 480's. I just shot a 190 Offhand in the State Service Rifle Championship. That's my best score ever and I am still improving. I also took the High Marine trophy. Thanks for the tip!" Richard Leech, Lake Geneva, Wisconsin

ANTICIPATING RECOIL

Figures 40 and 41 shows groups that indicate the shooter is anticipating the recoil of the rifle. If you fire an M-14, or most any rifle, with no sweatshirt, no shooting jacket, no sling, a loose grip and your head not placed firmly on the stock, IT WILL KICK THE HELL OUT OF YOU!!! Since you're smarter than that, you <u>can</u> overcome the recoil and you don't even notice it.

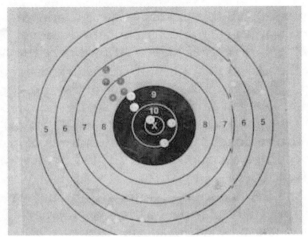

Figure 40
A typical group by a shooter who is anticipating the rifle recoil.

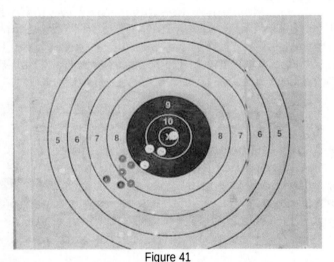

Figure 41
Figures 40 & 41 (above), are typical groups fired by a shooter who is anticipating recoil.

Always wear a sweatshirt (a hooded one is best) no matter what the temperature. The sweatshirt fills out the shooting jacket and maintains the body at an even temperature (HOT). It, along with the shooting jacket, helps absorb the recoil. In cold weather, a hooded sweatshirt is worth its weight in gold.

A good <u>leather</u> sling, properly adjusted (coming in the next book), will absorb most of the recoil. You must have a good firm grip and place your head firmly onto the stock. Your head will ride with the rifle as it recoils and it will not kick you. It just pushes your shoulder and you just ride with it. Your <u>concentration</u> should be so centered on sight alignment, focus and trigger control; you can ignore the recoil and just let it happen.

DRY FIRE

Dry firing is practice shooting without firing a live round. <u>NO AMMUNITION.</u> It is also called "snapping in". It can be done on the rifle range itself at the actual target. On a range, with the rifle pointed <u>down range</u>, is the only place you can dry fire unless there is a special area set up for that. The range will have some white signs, with different sized black circles, set up to indicate different distances.

You can also dry fire at home. Just make a black circle on a piece of paper and tape it to a wall. Make sure it is the size you need. When you look through the sights it should look the same as when you are on the range. When you dry fire, your routine must be the same as if you were live firing... except there is no ammunition in the firearm. Make sure you use <u>all</u> of your equipment. Have your hearing protector on and have your elevation on the sights. Forgetting these two items will cause you to place your head on the stock differently than you normally would.

HOLDING EXERCISES

When the Marine Corps Team picks up its members for the "Summer Team", they start the training program with holding exercises, a unique form of torture. Marines are in pretty good physical shape to start with and holding exercises train the body for the shooting sport. These exercises are done daily (Monday–Friday) for about six weeks. Holding exercises require a lot of self-discipline, except for Marines—they have a big, ugly Master Sergeant to act as their self-discipline.

Holding exercises require at least two people and it is best to work with a partner (less likely to quit). A wife or girl friend can help. The person playing the big, ugly Master Sergeant is the "caller" while the shooter does the exercises. The shooter sets up for the off-hand position, making sure he has <u>all </u>his gear set up. His scorebook is lying on his stool with a pen. Only one "caller" is needed, but any number of shooters can be on the line.

Once everyone is ready, the caller gets his stopwatch and calls "Prepare to Hold". The shooter gets his grip and places the rifle into his shoulder. The next command is "Hold" and the caller starts the watch. The shooter comes down into position and dry fires an off-hand shot. After the hammer falls, the shooter continues to hold the rifle in the off-hand position until the caller says, "Take them down". The time up is <u>one minute.</u>

The caller re-sets the stopwatch and gives the shooter a minute down. During the minute rest period the shooter picks up the pen and "calls his shot" in the data book. After one minute down, the caller again says, "Prepare to Hold".

The shooters do twenty holds, one minute up and one minute down. They then pair up for rapid-fire exercises. This is done daily for four to six weeks. It takes a lot of self-discipline, but it does help.

MENTAL CONDITIONING

A new shooter makes a lot of mistakes. The biggest is not focusing correctly. The next biggest mistake is "keeping score in your head". As you shoot, you count each point you have dropped. "I've got a 193 going"; after the next shot you think, "I've still got a 192," and so it goes. You have poor mental conditioning—I know, I've done the same thing. Chief Warrant Officer Nagazyna once told a young female Marine the best way to eliminate "keeping score in your head" was to get yourself a short stick, place it in your right boot and wrap your toes around it in the off-hand position. I tried his suggestion but it didn't work.

You have to stop the bad habits and start some good ones.

What I did about keeping score in my head was to ignore the score and talk to myself, under my breath of course. It makes other people nervous to see someone with a rifle talking to himself. Say, "This will be a center shot, a ten or an X," and repeat it over and over. After awhile you will get over the habit of keeping score in your head.

Henry Ford said "**If you think you can or if you think you can't—you are right!!!**" Everything you have learned or will learn about the mechanics of shooting is only 20% of the overall picture; <u>80% of shooting is mental conditioning.</u> The way you think and program your mind is the way you will shoot. If you think a ten or an X and do everything right, you will shoot a ten or an X. If you think a nine or think "out of the black", you still can do the mechanics right, but you will drop to a nine, or worse.

We were shooting a league match at 200 yards on the 600 yard reduced targets. During the string of twenty shots I thought, "a nine"—it flashed across my mind. I didn't want to break my rhythm, so I didn't stop and re-focus my mind and concentration. I thought a nine, and on my next shot I lost a point with a good call. My 199-16X was not as good as the other guy's 200-12X.

Start with the off-hand. Tell yourself, "This will be a center shot, a ten or X". Keep repeating it over and over. If a negative thought crosses your mind, <u>take the rifle down</u> and take that round out of the rifle. Start over with a new round.

Marine Corps Division "leg" Matches are fired over a two-day period. You fire twice across the course and the scores are added. The top ten percent of the non-Distinguished shooters receive either a Gold, Silver or Bronze medal. If you have never had "Match Pressure", the Marine Corps knows how to give it to you. They have a cute little device known as the "Rattle Board". It consists of a number of two-inch wide boards with information written with chalk; your name, rank, organization, all your scores <u>and</u> your current position in that match.

The first day across the course in the 1966 Eastern Division Matches was pretty uneventful for me. My name never even appeared on the rattle board. The second day of the match was another matter. I fired my twenty shots off-hand with no pressure; in fact I was almost in a daze. I fired exceptionally well. I gave no thought to looking at the "board". As we were moving back to the 300 yard line, a "<u>Friend</u> (?)" said, "Did you know that you are in position for 1st Gold?"

My eyes flew open, my heart stopped, my knees shook and my mind screamed, "FIRST GOLD!" I went back and looked at the rattle board. I swear that thing was seventy-five feet high and, sure enough, there on the top was my name. You could see my finger nails gripping the board, as I slipped from Gold to Silver, and finally, to hang in for a Bronze medal.

Wayne Anderson started High Power with some mechanical problems and received his classification of Marksman. He quickly had the problem fixed and started to shoot Master scores. He was soon reclassified as a Master and the Marksman class was happy to see him go. While at a fund raising dinner, I heard he had just received his High Master card. I started to think about the reaction from the Master class I had seen in the past. They were happy to see him go. Some people are happy to improve and others are just happy to get rid of the competition. It says a lot about the mental conditioning of each.

SETTING GOALS

A new shooter will set a goal, say, for the off-hand position. "I want to shoot a 190 off-hand". He may have a 180 average off-hand and he may reach his goal and start shooting 190's. But, he may be capable of higher scores when he sets his goal for 190, and shoots his way <u>down</u> to his goal. Concentration on each and every shot as a ten or an X, and let the score take care of itself.

In 1969 we shot a "Leg" match at Oak Ridge, TN. During the 300 yard rapid stage, a thunder storm passed over and soaked everyone. A bolt of lightning hit a field phone, knocking one of the Boy Scout volunteers working in the pits on his butt. All of the volunteers walked off, and a majority of the shooters quit. After the storm had abated, the match officials reorganized the few remaining shooters and finished the match. My whole team had quit. I was driving so they sat in the car as I finished the match. I won my second "Leg" Medal.

Even after a bad string of fire, the very fact that you hang in, and don't quit, can make the difference in winning or losing (See Figure 16).

Figure 16
Like the frog, if you give up—you lose.

When trying to improve your classification, set your goal <u>beyond</u> the one you want to reach. If you are an Expert, don't try for Master, go for High Master. You will be like the karate expert breaking the board. Think <u>through</u> Master. If you make High Master, GREAT. You will have met your goal. You may fall just short of High Master, but you will have made the <u>upper</u> end of Master class. That's far better than going for Master, and just making it, and ending up in the low end of the Master class.

Be careful – goals can become hurdles. I was a Master and I wanted to go for High Master, which is a score of 97 average for every ten shot string. I set my goal for 98 or 99 for every ten shot string. I made High Master, but soon found out it is <u>not</u> lonely at the top – it is crowded up there. A 98 or 99 average will keep you near the bottom of the High Master class. My goal became a hurdle, something to overcome. I had to set new goals, shooting 200's on a consistent basis.

I could not see myself going from the bottom of the High Master class to near the top overnight, but I could see it over a period of several years. I picked out people who were at the top and told myself I could shoot as well as them. I have caught up to and even passed a few. Re-setting the goals and knowing you can achieve them is the greatest step you can take. One day you will shoot a score that is far better than you have ever shot before. That will give you the confidence and knowledge; "I did it before and I can do it again!"

CHAPTER FIVE

ODDS & ENDS

In the Marine Corps, when we picked up a summer team and started to train the new shooters, the first thing we did after issuing the M-14's was to "mark the sights". One of the staff NCO's would bring his wife's or girlfriend's finger nail polish ("Street Walker Red" was the preferred color). Civilians seem to prefer white paint. Finger nail polish was used because it had to be removed at the end of the season.

When you look at the receiver, just below the rear sight on an M1A you will see some lines machined into both the receiver and the sight base see fig. 42. When the long center lines are lined up, the rifle is said to be on mechanical zero. Unless the light is just right, it is difficult to see the lines, and even when you can see them, the upper center line will be just to the left or right of the receiver line, and when you put on one click, it moves just to the right or left of the receiver line.

Fig. 42

MZO

Jim Owens

Mechanical Zero

Mechanical zero is the condition where there is **NO** elevation or windage, set on the rifle. To get the rifle to Mechanical zero start by turning the elevation knob(fig. 43) the knob on the left side of the sight base <u>Forward</u> until it is all the way **DOWN** and the sight is down into its well.

Fig. 43

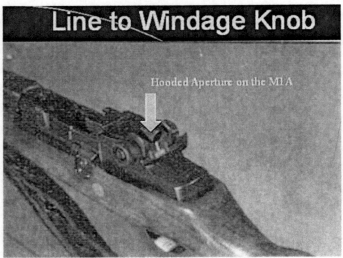

Fig. 44

The hooded aperture on the M1A has a "Notch" that shows if the sight is up or down. For Mechanical zero **Start With the notch DOWN.** By turning (Left or right) the notch to the up or 12 o'clock position you have added 1/2 minute of elevation to the rifle. By turning the notch down to the 6 o'clock position, you have removed 1/2 minute of elevation from the rifle.

The <u>Windage Mechanical zero</u> is when the long line of the movable sight base and the long line of the receiver are both lined up. That means there is an equal number of left and right clicks of windage available to the shooter.

Marking the Sights

Marking the sights is a six step procedure. In this case, let's use white paint, using a tooth pick or a fine tipped brush.

STEP ONE: Line up the two center lines on the back of the sight. If one is just a little off, don't worry, <u>that</u> becomes the mechanical zero. About a half inch to the <u>left</u> of the center lines paint a single straight line from the receiver base up and onto the sight base, much the same as the long center lines. Now do it again, about one half inch to the <u>right</u> of the center lines.

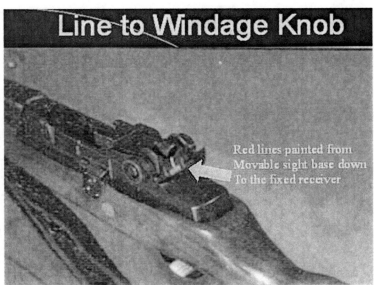

Fig. 45

STEP TWO: Look at the windage knob and the receiver next to it. From the top of the receiver, come back about an inch, and paint a line onto the receiver to the windage knob and across the edge of the windage knob. Now turn the rifle on its left side and continue to paint that line down to the center screw on the top of the windage knob.

Fig.46

This will do two things. First of all, when the rifle is set to the mechanical zero, you are 100% sure it is correct. The center lines will be lined up, as will the paint lines, <u>if</u> the line on the windage knob is lined up with the one on the receiver. If the lines are off on the knob, you know you are off one or two clicks. <u>**If lines on the windage knob do line up, and you are one full revolution off, the other three lines will be so far off that it will be instantly recognizable.**</u>

Fig. 47

Secondly, painting the line down to the center screw lets you know where the top mark is while you are shooting. If you are in the prone position and you have a couple of clicks on your rifle, you may forget exactly where it is set. You look up at the knob and cannot see the paint. By tilting the rifle to the left, you can see the painted line, down to the center screw, and <u>know</u> where the windage is set.

STEP THREE: Take the hooded rear sight and turn it to the 12 o'clock position. Paint a line across the top of the hooded sight from front to rear until it comes back to the V notch. During a string of rapid fire as the coach says come up or down one half of a minute, you don't want to waste valuable time looking for that V notch – the paint stands out.

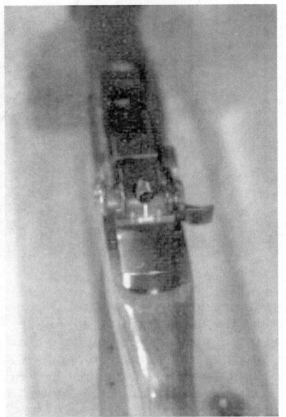

Fig. 48

STEP FOUR: Run the elevation knob all the way down and paint a line on the elevation knob, and then, from the knob onto the receiver, just like you did on the windage knob. You do not have to paint the knob on its side down to the center screw. When the shooter is ready for his string of fire and he glances down, and sees the two lines on the elevation knob lined up, he knows he forgot to put his elevation on the rifle. He just hopes it's not a rapid fire string as the targets are coming up.

STEP FIVE: Paint a line on the gas cylinder plug, downward and onto the gas cylinder. When I first started shooting the M-14, my gas cylinder plug came loose. I took it over to the armorer and he noticed that it was not marked. He tightened it down, marked it and said, "You will have to re-zero the rifle." The next day, after re-zeroing the rifle, I went to write in my 600 yard line elevation and it was <u>TEN FULL MINUTES</u> different than the day before. If it had been marked, the change would have been only one or one half of a minute.

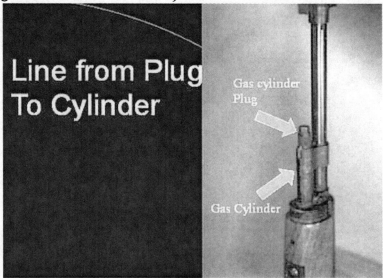

Fig. 49

STEP SIX: This must wait until after the shooter zeros the rifle at 200 yards, and the front sight is adjusted, and the windage zero is no more than two clicks right or left of the mechanical zero. We fired a 1000 yard match at Twenty Nine Palms, CA. The wind was so strong; I used 32 clicks of left wind <u>and</u> aimed at my left upright. You want to be close to mechanical zero. You never know when you will need those extra clicks of windage. After the rifle has been zeroed and the front sight adjusted, paint a line on the front sight itself, starting from the sight down to the base on which it sits. Do this at the <u>front</u> end, near the flash suppressor, so you don't see it as you look through the sights. If the screw should ever come loose and your front sight falls off, all you have to do is put it back and line up the two lines and tighten the screw – This should put you within one half minute of your zero.

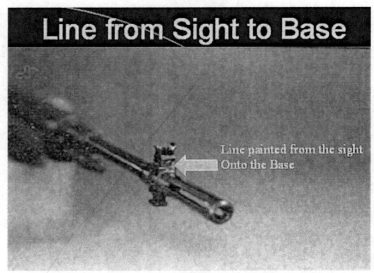

Fig. 50

ZEROING

During a Wednesday night practice, at 600 yards, I had just finished my string and had a little time. So I quickly put on my new Leupold 24 power scope and tried to get on paper. Zeroing from 600 yards, with no assistance, no down range settings and no time to bore sight, is <u>NOT</u> a good idea. (No one ever accused me of being smart!) I fired a few shots and was not on paper. I tried shooting high, low, left and right. I was running low on ammunition. Finally, I hit paper. "I know what to do now," I thought. I came up the correct number of clicks and fired again. The target came up and the spotter was only inches from the last shot. I was totally surprised and again, I came up the correct number of clicks. Again, the target came up with the spotter only inches from the last shot. Panic is starting to set in and, for the third time I came up the correct number of clicks and, for the third time, the spotter was in the same place. I was out of ammunition and was looking at my new scope with total horror, when I heard, "ah-hum". I looked over to the next firing point, and Eric Obermeyer was still in the prone position, with his elbow on the ground, and his chin resting on the palm of his hand, grinning at me.

"What!?!"

"*Well*, you were shooting on my target, so I thought I would shoot on yours."

I closed my eyes, dropped my chin to my chest, and counted to ten. It didn't help – I was still out of ammunition.

Back to the M1A. The rifle has a mechanical zero, that is your starting point. You should return to the mechanical zero <u>after each string of fire</u> and record that setting (Your "No Wind Zero") in your data book. If the number of clicks on the elevation knob are less than your normal zero, it could mean your elevation knob is loose and/or your sights are "running down". Mechanical zero has two settings: elevation (Up & Down) and windage (Left & Right). The elevation knob is moved toward the front of the rifle so the sight is clicked down until it can go no further. The hooded sight is turned so the V notch is in the <u>down</u> position. If it is up, you have one half minute elevation on the rifle.

The hooded rear sight gives you the luxury of adding half minute clicks to a full minute elevation knob, by simply rotating the hooded sight up or down. The center of the aperture, or hole, is offset from the center of the sight just a little. When the V notch is in the up position, the center of the aperture is just above the center of the sight. When you rotate it down, the center of the aperture moves to just below the center of the sight. This gives you the half minute adjustment. A little later, I'll cover the use of the hooded rear sight. With both the elevation knob and the V notch down, the line on the windage knob lined up with the one on the receiver, and all three lines on the back of the receiver lined up, you are at the mechanical zero, or your starting point.

A "No Wind" Zero

To hit the center of the target, you must have a good no wind zero. The zero is the amount of elevation and windage for:

1. Each yard line

2. Each position

3. The light conditions

69

4. The ammunition used

5. The range you are on.

Both the Off-Hand and Sitting Rapid are fired from 200 yards and each position may require its own zero. Some people have the same setting for both; most people will have a different setting.

Moving back to other yard lines requires new settings. More elevation is needed to compensate for bullet drop, and the windage zero may change as well. On some rifles, the sight does not come straight out of the well; it makes a slight angle, so you have to add clicks of windage at each yard line. I had one rifle which used settings of two left at 200 yards, "MZ" (mechanical zero) at 300 yards and three right at 600 yards.

The time of day will have an effect on your zero because of light conditions. The incident that really got my attention happened on a Saturday afternoon, shooting 1000 yards. While at Lodi, WI the sun in the late afternoon comes from the ranges 12 o'clock position, straight into the shooters face. It was early afternoon, so the sun was not shining in my face. I had a new sight, but not a new sight base, so my elevation knob was <u>all</u> the way to its uppermost limit, and I was hitting center. The next morning, the sun was behind us. With the sight still set all the way up, I was hitting six o'clock, in the six-ring. I had no more mechanical elevation to click on, so I had to aim above the target, at the number board, and come down some to hit the black. Granted, this was an extreme case, but light can and will affect your zero.

Now that you can use your own ammunition in DCM Leg Matches (Now CMP), Distinguished badges are going to be cheaper, the shooter no longer has to "Look" for a zero for the ammo, now that he can use his own. In the "Old Days" we were issued ammunition. When you changed "lots" of ammunition you changed your zero. When manufactures of ammunition make a Batch or "Lot" of ammo, the characteristics of each batch or lot most likely will give you a "Zero Shift." There are no Sighters in CMP Leg Matches.

The rifle range you are on affects your zero, mainly due to the light. If you go to a different range, expect a zero change.

All of the above is true and most people will agree. Now, I'm going to tell you something that is my own conclusion, garnered from my over 45 years of experience. I'm not sure others will agree with me. Some people think their zero for a given yard line and position is hard and fast – set in concrete. They don't care if they are hitting wide nines, or eights at one o'clock; **their zero** is ten and thirty-seven sixty-fourths up, and nineteen sixty-fourths right. (That's a joke, Pat).

I would be interested in knowing where they got the sixty-fourths minute sights. I have found, particularly with the Service Rifle, my zero stayed close to a given setting, but it "floated", or changed daily, for any number of reasons, and sometimes for no reason at all.

After weeks of practice in a Division Leg Match, on the old 5V target, the first shot for record Off-Hand (Standing), on the day of the match, was a high four at 12 o'clock. I called the shot good, came down two full minutes, and ran the next nineteen shots in the black. I accepted the zero change and made it, without breaking my stride to try and figure out why.

If you do have a change, make sure you "carry it back" to all other positions. Make the same changes at all yard lines.

Zeroing the rifle should happen on the 200 yard line, with a helper spotting for you, and from the most stable position you will be using. (Usually prone is the most stable position) In most competition matches, you do not shoot the prone position from 200 yards. You should zero from the sitting position, because that is the most stable position you will be using at that yard line. If you want to "wimp out", you can use the prone position to get yourself on paper and centered up, but know in advance, that when you change positions you will have to change your zero.

On some rifles, the amount of sling tension put on the rifle can "warp the barrel" just enough to change the zero. The M-16A1 is definitely subject to sling tension problems! They straightened the barrel on the A2, but it's still subject to small amounts of "warping". Some people zero their rifle from a bench rest or sand bags. The rifle is perfectly centered <u>until</u> they stand up and try to shoot. They find themselves off by as much as 10-12 inches.

Some points to remember: (1) with some rifles, the slightest pressure will cause the barrel to warp. (2) Never shoot with the barrel against a solid object. It will shoot in the opposite direction from the point of contact. For example, if you rest the barrel against a fence post on the left side it will shoot to the right.   (3) More important, when you bench a rifle it disturbs the harmonics. Don't ask me to explain. All I know is if you disturb a harmonic it will turn and bite you!

When you are on the 200 yard line and in the Sitting Position and are ready to go, put about ten to twelve minutes of elevation on the rifle and leave the windage on mechanical zero. With some experience, you can look at the height of the front sight and estimate the number of clicks to start with. Have the spotter stand by, with his scope set up above and behind you, so the axis of his scope is over the axis of your barrel. He should have communications with the pits and a <u>7/64</u> inch Allen wrench used to move the front sight if need be.

When you tell the spotter you are ready to go, he should watch through his scope for the break of the bullet as you shoot. You will fire one shot and the pits will tell you weather or not you are on paper, and if you are high, low, left or right. Make your adjustments on the sights (the <u>amount</u> of adjustments will be covered in the next chapter). **Remember, turning the windage knob forward, or away from you, moves the strike of the bullet to the right and turning it back, towards you, moves the strike of the bullet to the <u>left</u>**.

I was watching a movie called "Uncommon Valor." A guy was zeroing an M-1 Garand. His spotter called "High and Right," twice. The shooter moved his windage knob <u>forward</u>, which moves the strike of the bullet to the right. If he is hitting "High and Right," he should come down and LEFT. To move the strike of the bullet left he should move the windage knob <u>BACK</u> towards him.

Once the shot is on paper, tell the pits you will fire a <u>three</u>

shot group. After they mark the group, move the sights off the center of the group, provided you called all three shots good. Move the elevation knob as needed, but keep in mind: you want at least six minutes of elevation, minimum, to compensate for conditions later and no more than fifteen minutes of elevation. You want to make sure that you have enough elevation to shoot long range matches up to 1000 yards. If you have more than fifteen minutes, a gunsmith can cut the front sight down for you. It must be cut even and square. With less than six minutes of elevation, you should replace the front sight.

If your shot group is more than two clicks to the right or left of mechanical zero, have your spotter loosen the screw on your front sight with the Allen wrench. Move the sight "into" the direction of the strike of the bullet.

If the **group is to the right** of the aiming black by more than two clicks, **move the front sight to the right** a small amount. It doesn't take much. Remember to tighten down the screw on the front sight and return the windage knob back to mechanical zero, prior to taking your next three shot group.

After you have centered your group (both elevation and windage), make sure the screw is tight, mark the sight with the paint, (in case it ever comes loose) and record the elevation and windage in your data book.

Keep in mind that you shot these groups slow fire and your sitting string will be rapid fire. You may have a slight change. When you stand up for Off-Hand, you may also have a slight change.

NORMAL COME UPS

You should memorize "The normal come ups", not only for yourself, but to help a new shooter who has never fired beyond 200 yards. Normal come ups are designed for *one thing only*: to give you a number of full minute clicks from a given yard line to the next, to get your shot "ON PAPER". It is not designed to get your shot from the center of the X ring at a given yard line to the center of the X ring at the next yard line. *This is a rule of thumb*, and it applies to all types of rifles and ammunition used in competitive high power shooting. It probably will not apply to your uncle's .975 cal. Submarine hunting rifle. (Another joke, Pat)

The normal come up from the 200 yard line to the 300 yard line is <u>three</u> full minutes. That is three additional minutes to the elevation you already have on the rifle for your 200 yard zero. For me that three minutes is exactly perfect, center X to center X. You may have to use more or less, but you will be on paper for your first shot.

The normal come up from 300 yards to 600 yards is <u>twelve</u> minutes.

The normal come up from 600 yards to 1000 yards is <u>twenty-two</u> minutes. Remember, these are additional minutes to the number of clicks already on the rifle at 600 yards. The first time I met Sgt. Maj. Steve Allerman was on the 800 yard line at Lodi, WI. He said he had never fired beyond 600 yards before and didn't know what to use. I did a few calculations using normal come ups and gave him a starting point. His first shot was in the ten ring. It impressed the hell out of him.

Remember each sight has a different number of clicks that equal a minute. Put a piece of tape on the rifle and write it down.

When I learned the normal come ups, I was taught:
 200 yards to 300 yards = +3 minutes
 300 yards to 600 yards = +11 minutes
 600 yards to 1000 yards = +22 minutes

Nothing was ever said about the normal come ups from 600 yards to 800 yards, 800 yards to 900 yards and 900 yards to 1000 yards. I can only give you what works for me. My zero from 600 yards to 800 yards is <u>ten</u> minutes, from 800 yards to 900 yards is <u>six</u> minutes and from 900 yards to 1000 yards is <u>six</u> minutes. These three numbers do total twenty-two minutes; the normal come up from 600 yards to 1000 yards.

Some years ago, Boots Obermeyer and I were sitting behind the ready line at 200 yards and a new shooter came up to Boots and said, "I've never shot anywhere but 200 yards. What amount should I come up for the 300 yard?" "Three minutes" immediately jumped into my mind.

Boots started to ask him a number of questions: "What caliber rifle are you shooting? What weight bullet? What powder are you using? How many grains of powder?" I thought, "Wow, I'm going to learn something new," and about that time came the answer, "three minutes should get you on paper." That's when I learned Boots has a mischievous streak in him.

OLD TIME SHOOTER COME UPS

An "Old Timer" shooter gave me a formula for come ups from 0 (the target) to 1,000 yards in increments of 100 yards. The formula is **"2-2-3-3-4-4-5-5-6-6"**. Simply put:

1. From the target to 100 yds = **2** min.
2. From 100 yds to 200 yds = **2** min.
3. From 200 yds to 300 yds = **3** min.
4. From 300 yds to 400 yds = **3** min.
5. From 400 yds to 500 yds = **4** min.
6. From 500 yds to 600 yds = **4** min.
7. From 600 yds to 700 yds = **5** min.
8. From 700 yds to 800 yds = **5** min.
9. From 800 yds to 900 yds = **6** min.
10..From 900 yds to 1,000 yds = **6** min.

Look at the numbers from 600 yds to 1,000 yds, they add up to **22** mins., that's the same number we used 35 years ago. Remember "Normal Come Ups" are to get you on paper; you need to adjust to the center once you are on paper.

LIGHT EFFECTS

Sunlight has a strange sense of humor when it comes to shooting. As a child, it learned a trick called optical illusions. Two people can look at the same optical illusion and see it in different ways. Have you ever seen the one of a group of squares or blocks stacked in a corner? Someone else will see it as a stack of blocks floating in mid-air and coming toward you. After they explain it, you then can see what they see, if you make your mind do a leap. This is called "Perspective".

The first example, Figure 51, is of the front sight post. The large rectangle is the whole front sight post. The sun has washed out the side that is slightly shaded and the shooter sees only the solid black rectangle. Thinking he sees the full front sight post, he then centers that portion on the six o'clock position of the aiming black (shown here by the solid black circle). He really is shaded to the right of the aiming black, so his shot goes slightly to the right. The shot is shown by the small white circle.

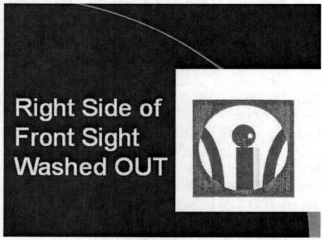

Figure 51
A bright light from the side will cause the front sight to appear narrower and cause your shots to go toward the light.

Another illusion is shown in Figure 52. The sun has washed out the top of the front sight post, so the shooter pushes the sight into the aiming black, to what he thinks is the six o'clock position. His shot then goes high. Both of these illusions can be minimized by blackening the sights with the carbide lamp.

Figure 52

A strong light from above causes the front sight to appear shorter and, in turn, will cause your shots to go high.

The sun has been around a long time, and a little thing like a carbide lamp is NOT going to spoil its fun. It has an optical illusion that messes with your target. To some people it appears that the aiming black is <u>larger</u> than the actual size, while to others it appears <u>smaller</u> than the actual size.

Figure 53 shows the black appearing larger than normal. The white line inside the circle represents the actual aiming black. The black area outside that circle shows the optical illusion as seen by the shooter. He puts his front sight post at what he thinks is the six o'clock position; his sight and shot is low.

Figure 53

Prevailing light conditions may cause the target to appear larger. Your zero will cause your shots to go low.

Figure 54 shows the illusion as the black looking smaller than normal. The outside black line is the actual aiming black and the black circle is what the shooter sees. The rest is washed out. The shooter places the post at what he thinks is the six o'clock position; the post and the shot is high. Both illusions can be handled by using a center hold. Center is center. You may be one of the many people that the light does not affect, but then again, you may be one of the people it does affect. You should know the different effects and how to deal with them.

Figure 54
Prevailing light conditions may cause the black to appear smaller than normal. With the zero on the rifle, your shots will go high.

CHAPTER SIX

DON'T BLAME THE BARREL MAKER (OR THE GUNSMITH)

I KNOW A LOT OF PEOPLE WHO LOVE TO LISTEN TO Boots Obermeyer and Jack Krieger talk. I am one of them. Not only are they two of the best barrel makers in the country, they have a wealth of knowledge of all aspects of the shooting sport. *It has been said that a dog understands one seventh of what is being said: for the rest he nods his head and wags his tail. I know how that dog feels.* When Boots and Jack start talking they tend to slip into the language with which they are most comfortable. It is TECHNOLOGICAL-ESE, which leaves the rest of us very interested, but nodding our heads and wagging our tails. This puppy shall attempt to explain the one seventh he does understand to the rest of us mongrels.

I have heard each of them say, more than once, they will send out a new barrel, and in less than a month, the customer is yelling that the barrel does not shoot at all. When they have him bring the barrel in, the "Crown" is damaged from improper care and cleaning.

I never knew much about the crown until I met Charlie Milazzo, Gunsmith Extraordinaire. I gave Charlie one of my old barrels to use on his hunting rifle. He put it aside and didn't even look at it for a couple of years. I've heard Charlie preach on barrel crowns for years, but it never sank in. I once told him, "Everyone has a purpose in life, even if it is only to be used as a bad example." He thinks it is hilarious to use my old barrel as the bad example. I **do** have a contract out **on him**.

WHAT IS THE RIFLE CROWN?

The rifle crown is on the muzzle end of the rifle. The muzzle is where the bullet leaves the barrel. The idea is to have the escaping gases will come out in a perfect uniform pattern, equally around the bullet. To protect the rifle crown, it is set back or recessed a little. Some crowns are tapered, beveled or radiused, but they all allow the gasses to escape in a uniform pattern around the exiting bullet. Figure 55 shows a good crown and Figure 56 shows a damaged crown.

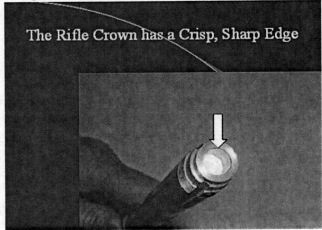

Figure 55 Example of a good rifle crown.

Figure 56 Example of a bad rifle crown.

Using your imagination, let's look inside the rifle. When the hammer falls and hits the primer, which explodes and causes the powder to burn rapidly which builds up to 50,000 pounds per square inch inside the cartridge and this pressure pushes the bullet down the barrel. there is an "explosion" inside the cartridge—50,000 lbs per square inch. Don't worry, the rifle barrel can handle it. We had a guy in boot camp that couldn't shoot because that figure 50,000 pounds per square inch freaked him out.

The gases push in all directions; the brass expands and grips the wall of the chamber; the head of the case stretches to the rear a fraction of an inch and is stopped by the bolt and locking system. The gases take the path of least resistance and propel the bullet forward. The bullet "jumps" into the lands and grooves (more on that later).

"**Break**" – I know that you know all of this. I need to start from a point of common knowledge and work up to the point where everyone will learn something new. Please bear with me and read on.

The barrel's lands and grooves are spiraled and they start the bullet rotating as the bullet travels down the length of the barrel. This rotation is what gives the bullet its stability while in flight to its target. Ideally, the bullet will rotate on its axis. If anything should cause the bullet to rotate just a little off of its axis, the bullet will have a slight "wobble", and this will significantly affect it's accuracy. It is not so much at short ranges, but the longer the range, the worse it gets. A larger wobble just makes things worse.

Now to the crown. What people consider normal care and cleaning, Charlie considers "Rifle Abuse". Cleaning the rifle from the muzzle end, which must be done with the M-1 and the M-14, requires <u>extreme</u> care. The cleaning rod can "ding" the crown. Ding is a low technological term and may not be understood by some technocrats. Don't think, *"Because the rifle barrel is made of steel, you can't hurt it"* – it <u>doesn't take much</u>.

ANATOMY OF A DING

When the cleaning rod strikes the crown, creating the ding, it usually occurs when using a rifle rod that is screwed together, or at the joint where the brush or patch holder screws into the rod itself. Two things happen: First, metal rolls over into the barrel, causing a miniature speed bump for the oncoming bullet. The bullet has just reached a speed of 2,700 feet per second. That is a half-mile per second or about 1,800 miles per hour. If you don't think a speed bump can have an effect, try driving your car over one at 20 mph.

Second, the crown receives a little cut or groove due to the dirt outside of the cleaning rod or an abrasion from the cleaning rod and dirt, repeatedly rubbing on the inside edge of the bore. This allows the gases to escape in an uneven pattern and has the effect of slightly tipping the bullet off its axis as it rotates, creating the wobble. As an example, like an air plane that hits a sudden cross wind, it yaws or turns to the side.

One little ding will not cause great accuracy loss, but the more you shoot, the more you clean the rifle. Without extreme care, you will have more dings, <u>and they add up FAST!</u>

WHAT SHOULD YOU DO?

First, <u>NEVER</u> use a steel or aluminum rod that comes in multiple sections; more joints equals more dings. Charlie wants to take everyone who uses one, shave his head, and send him to Boot Camp! However, I pointed out that boot camp is where the problem originated. Always use a one piece <u>coated</u> cleaning rod.

Stay away from fiberglass rods they can actually take the lands and grooves out of the rifle. Several years ago while working with muzzleloaders several manufacturers make work rods out of fiberglass and after 6 months it was discovered that these rods were wearing out the lands and grooves. So the manufactures began coating the fiberglass rods. This solved the problem. There many of these rods made for black powder and some were made for modern rifle and pistols and the same thing happened. Not all of the fiberglass rods were taken off the market or coated. They are still out there—be careful.

When cleaning the M1 or M-14 from the muzzle, always use a rod guide and make sure you wipe the rod with a clean rag each time you send it down the bore. Leave the patch holder off and carefully feed the end of the rod into the bore, being careful not to touch the crown. Now carefully rotate the rod as you screw the patch holder and patch, with cleaning solvent, onto the rod. The reason for wiping down the rod is to prevent rotating grit in the barrel. Now, <u>pull </u>the rod out the barrel; never push into the barrel. Do not stroke the rod back and forth inside the barrel. Modern solvents do the job chemically; you don't need the scrubbing action.

You are not safe from dings on the crown just because you have a bolt gun or an AR-15, with which you can remove the bolt and clean from the rear. Take it from "the bad example!" I pushed the rod through the bore and pulled it back. The holder on the end of the rod would ding the crown. My barrel is now giving Charlie a good laugh.

Jack Krieger and Charlie Milazzo have developed a theory. If you use REMCLEAN, which is a mild abrasive, and you push the patch through the bore, it is a very tight fit and cleans very well. As the patch exits the muzzle, it expands. You should <u>not</u> pull the patch back into the bore past the crown. Pulling it back compresses the patch again and the REMCLEAN, which is like a very fine sand paper, causes a wear pattern on the crown, not to mention the possibility of a ding. Frankly, the REMCLEAN polishes the crown such that any dings are smoothed out, making the damage to the crown harder to detect. It is still there—you can be sure! **<u>Push</u>** the rod through and take off the patch. **<u>Never</u>** pull it back!

It may take a little longer to clean the rifle, and you will go through a few more patches, but the savings on the crown will extend the life of your barrel, and more importantly, the accuracy. If you don't pay attention, you can pay for a re-crowning and in some cases where the barrel cannot be re-crowned, then you will need a new barrel. But "don't blame the barrel maker."

My scores have increased tremendously over the past couple of years. When you make High Master, the increases become more and more difficult. You have to work harder for a single point or X increase. That single point or X can be the difference in winning or losing. I found myself in a position where 85-90% of my shots were going where I wanted them. I was, however, having fliers — shots outside the normal pattern, unexplained. These fliers were particularly evident at the longer ranges, 600 yards and 1000 yards.

During a few of my marathon gab-fests with Charlie Milazzo, I learned that, other than the crown damage, there were other probable causes to my fliers. Two of them are "Throat Erosion" and "Bullet Run Out". After much learning and many corrections, my fliers have been considerably reduced. I hear again and again, "That's fine for you as a High Master, but for me and my Marksman friends, we wouldn't notice the difference". I tell them, "You may experience the same problems I did; the difference is, **some** of the fliers you blame on yourself are really something mechanical, and they **can be** corrected!!"

THROAT EROSION

When the bullet leaves the chamber to be hurled down the bore, and rotated by the lands and grooves, it must first jump through the area known as the "**Throat**." This is a slight taper leading to the lands and grooves. The bullet leaves the neck of the cartridge and makes a "jump" through the throat to engage the lands and grooves.

"The smaller the jump or "Free Bore," the greater the accuracy, and the fewer the fliers." **That is not true. Yes, I did write that in the Blue book, but I have learned new information since then. There is a "Sweet Spot" that must be found, actually there are several "Sweet Spots," one of the sweet spots could be 10 thousandths off the lands and a second sweet spot could be forty-thousandths off the lands. Once you find one of the sweet spots, your Long Range groups will shrink tremendously.**

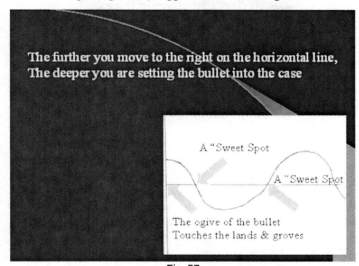

Fig. 57
There is a "Sweet Spot" that will give you the best group. There can be "More Than One" sweet spot

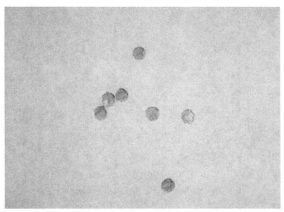

Fig. 58
This 1st picture is .005 before a sweet spot.

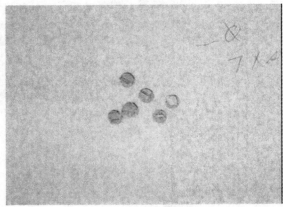

Fig. 59
This 2nd picture is on the sweet spot.

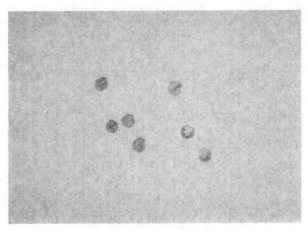

Fig. 60
This 3rd picture is .005 after the sweet spot.

- In my one week class, I teach you how to find the sweet spot.

You should not have the bullet touch the lands, and have no jump, because this condition can cause <u>excessive</u> or inconsistent pressure. The excessive pressure could be dangerous, and inconsistent pressure is not conducive to optimum accuracy.

The amount of jump, or free bore, in the Rapid Fire stages

<u>must</u> be rather large. The bullets are seated into the cartridge necks deep enough to insure: (1) that they will fit into the magazine for the service rifles, and, (2) that they will feed into the well when fed by stripper clips on a bolt rifle. Fortunately, the Rapid Fire stages are held at closer ranges and the problem is not significant.

With a new barrel, that hasn't been broken in, the free bore is rather small. You may start with your bullets set fairly deeply into the cartridge case and there is no problem.

Being fat, dumb and happy, I never knew there was a problem until I talked with Charlie. I thought those fliers were my fault. I found out that as you shoot more and more rounds, the throat wears, and it becomes larger. The more rounds you have fired, the more the bullet has to jump. I also found that using a heavier bullet, something I like to do, causes the throat to wear even faster.

I would like to take a minute and make a public apology to all the Marine Corps Armorers. They were always after me to keep up my <u>yellow book "record of rounds fired"</u> that was issued with each rifle. I never did. Now I know the importance of keeping that record. I now keep a log of my rounds fired in my Data Book., every time I shoot, the number of shots fired is recorded. The Jim Owens Data Books have this log in the back of the book. It is a great tool.

Fig. 61

Charlie has taught me that as the throat wears and the bullet has a longer jump, you have to seat your bullets out longer, to reduce the amount of free bore. Most of the rounds will make the jump just fine, but some of the bullets have slight imperfections within the core. As the bullet makes the longer jump, the center of mass is slightly off. This is why you check your bullets when you reload for evenness and roundness. Even though it will go down the barrel spinning, it will not spin on its true axis. It will have a slight "wobble" as it leaves the barrel. As little as a thousand rounds through the rifle can cause enough throat erosion to cause the problem. It can be measured.

WHAT CAN YOU DO?

I was shown a method, using a cleaning rod and a couple of stop collars, to determine the overall length of seating for my bullets and to monitor the throat erosion. The method does work. I discovered a potential safety hazard; however, I will not take the time to discuss it here. Fortunately, I did run into Tom Peterson from Stoney Point Products and he showed me his "Chamber-All" or OAL (Over All Length) Gauge. It was featured in the December 1992 *AMERICAN RIFLEMAN*, page 13. I was quite impressed with the gauge - see Figure 62. The basic OAL- gauge & a modified case to fit your caliber rifle. (You can get other caliber cases, which screw onto the gauge.)

Note; The OAL-Straight, The OAL-Curved, The Bullet Comparator, V-block Used to check bullet run out and Competition Seating Die can all be purchased from Sinclair International, 800-717-6211

Fig. 62

The nice thing about the gauge is that you use the same bullets you are going to be shooting. I use different weight bullets at each yard line and the seating depth is different for each. To use the gauge, you simply remove the bolt from the rifle. This gauge works only on rifles where the bolt can be removed and the gauge can be inserted from the rear, or chamber end, i.e., bolt rifles and the AR-15. Mr. Peterson has perfected **a curved gauge that will work on the M 1A and M-1 Garand**.

Pull the rod the entire way back, insert a bullet into the neck of the case, and make sure it goes down into the case. Place the case into the chamber and push the rod forward. The rod will push the bullet forward until the bullet touches the lands. Tighten the thumbscrew to hold the rod in place and remove the gauge. If the bullet sticks in the lands, simply tap it out with a cleaning rod, being careful of the barrel's crown. Place the bullet back into the neck and simply measure the overall length from the tip of the bullet to the bottom of the case with a dial caliper.

Remember, this length is where the bullet touches the lands, and this length gives the excessive pressure. You will want to seat the bullet a little deeper into the case, so you set your seating die a few thousandths shorter than this measurement. How much shorter? I read one article that said 3 to 5 thousandths. I tried that and boy did I get in trouble. I made my measurement and set my die for 3 thousandths deeper and started to seat a bunch of bullets. I don't just set the die, take three or four measurements, and then run the batch. I measure <u>every</u> round, and I have found that every seating die I've tried will not seat to an exact amount. They will seat to an acceptable range. Charlie says, "It's not the fault of the die, the bullets do not have uniform tips, the ogives <u>are</u> uniform and that's where measurements should be taken." Tips don't have to be perfect to give good accuracy, but the bases do. Figure 63 shows a tool made by Tom Peterson called the "bullet comparator" and it attaches to your dial caliper. It measures the seating depth off the ogive and not the tip.

When I first got the "Bullet Comparator" I did a little experiment. I had ten (10) .308 loaded rounds, so I used my old method of measuring them with my dial caliper (From the tip of the round to the base). I got .012 thousandths variation on the lengths. I then placed the bullet comparator body on the dial caliper and inserted the .308 insert. I then measured the same ten rounds. <u>The bullet comparator measures off the ogive of the bullet and not the tip</u>. I got .001 thousand variation from the same ten rounds. I was impressed.

Fig. 63
Over-all length gauge and bullet comparator

I had one round that would not seat down to the proper depth so I set it aside. At the end of that lot, I set it deeper and kept setting it deeper until it measured the same as the others. I used it as my first sighter and thought my rifle had blown up!! I was lucky it hadn't. Smoke came out of the floor plate; the primer was blown out. I now measure every round and, if it will not seat to within the range I want, it goes in the discard pile.

I use 15-20 thousandths as my free bore, or jump, and it works pretty well. Remember to re-check the overall length after every thousand rounds, more often if you use 220 gr. bullets. As the throat erodes, seat your bullets out to the new length and it will help eliminate those fliers.

BULLET RUN OUT

I started to pay attention to throat erosion and seating depth, but I was still getting fliers. Charlie said, "How about your bullet run out?" I told him, "I may be so ugly, my mother had to tie a pork chop around my neck to get the dog to play with me, but I've never had a bullet run out on me yet." I opened my mouth too soon. Then I found out what bullet run out was.

In the final stages of hand loading, you place a bullet into the neck of the case; run the press up and the die "seats" the bullet. In a perfect world, the bullet would be seated dead center into the neck of the case and, when fired, would rotate on its axis as it goes down the barrel. There would be no wobble. The die seldom seats the bullet dead center. It is off by varying amounts, which can be measured. This is usually the fault of the brass and can be encountered even when using precision seating dies.

A bullet that is really bad may be placed on a flat surface (like a table) and you will see the tip wobble as you roll the case. If the bullet is that bad, you could have a seven or six at 600 yards and think it is your "poor" shooting ability.

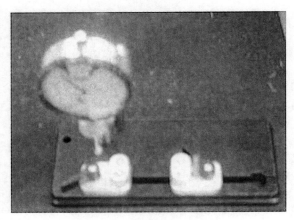

Fig. 64
V-block Used to check bullet run out.

WHAT ARE YOU WILLING TO ACCEPT?

The shooter who loads his own ammunition without checking for run out, either doesn't know about it or is willing to accept things as they are. We see some shooters who think a six-inch group at 100 yards is just great ("That's the best I've ever shot!"). We know we can do better. Run out becomes important at long ranges, so we have to set a maximum range or maximum run out we will accept. Charlie says, "For national match shooting, no more than six thousandths". My standard is four thousandths.

You have to have a way to check for run out, to know how much you have. Figure 64 is a block sold by Sinclair International (260-493-7104).

The dial indicator is placed to ride on the bullet at the "Ogive," the part that starts sloping down to the tip. You can rotate the dial until it reads zero or read it from any point on the dial. You are looking for the combined number of thousandths of an inch above and below the starting point. You need to rotate the case rather quickly and watch the needle move.

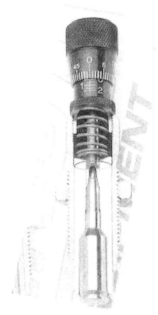

Fig. 65

I got a <u>real</u> education when I tested my hand loads. The ones that had six thousandths run out were my **good** ones. I was getting 8, 10, 12, and 15 thousandths run out. Someone told me, "If you set the bullet in the neck, run the case one halfway into the die, stop, rotate the case within the shell holder, then finish seating the bullet, it will help." Not enough for my money.

With the standard seating die I was using, I was getting 50% of my loads at 6-12 thousandths run out — *not acceptable.* I ordered a "Competition Seating Die" (The kind with a micrometer adjustment on top see fig. 65) and 100% of my loads became within six thousandths or less.

I still check all of my rounds. I find some rounds have zero run out and 1-2 thousandths is common. Any rounds over four thousandths are used for practice or close range.

Jim Owens

What the hell is a Meplat?

The short answer is, the ragged tip of a hollow point bullet. So, why is it important? Listen up, this is **really** important.

We had a bolt-gun shooter show up at a match, only to discover he had all his bullets seated out for long range. They were too long to fit in the receiver for rapid fire. He took a flat file and he filed off the tips of the bullets and made the rounds short enough to fit into the receiver. He shot 100–7X.

Another shooter did the same thing by loading his rounds too long. He did not have a file, so he placed each round, one at a time on, the cement and tapped the tip of the bullet with a hammer, into the case to make them shorter. He fired a 100–3X.

Nowadays there is a much better way. There is now a tool that trims the meplat. The funny part is, **the advantages are more for Long Range ammo**. Actually it works great for 300 yards and at longer distances. It has little or no affect at 200 yards or shorter. In fact the further back you shoot the better it works.

The advantages are: 1) the groups are smaller and rounder, anywhere from 15% to 45% smaller than the non-trimmed bullets. 2) trimmed bullets have less flyers.

This sounds too good to be true. I had a class with 10 students so I decided to see for myself. I had each of the 10 people shoot a 10 shot string with the untrimmed bullets and another 10 shot string with the trimmed bullets. I had them do this both at 300 yards and again at 600 yards.

I took each person's data book and I accurately plotted each string before trimming and after trimming, again at both 300 yards and again at 600 yards. **Guess what – it works as advertised.** The groups with the trimmed bullets were smaller and rounder. Some were about 10% to 15% smaller and some groups were about 40% to 45% smaller. The tips of the bullets look like someone had cut them off with a meat cleaver. The tool itself can use different inserts for the caliper you want to use. See the before and after pictures.

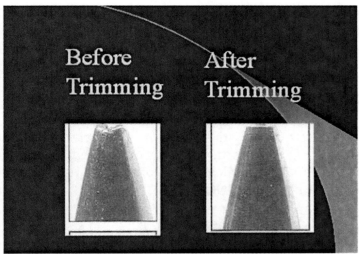

Fig. 66

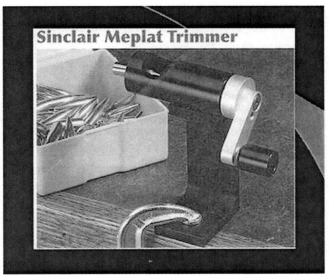

Fig. 67

Okay, where can I get this wonder tool? Once again Sinclair International 260-493-7104.

Keep in mind, this works on hollow point bullets. It does not work for the plastic tip ones like the A–Max bullets.

Between getting the correct seating depth to find your

"Sweet Spot" and trimming the meplat's, you will have a huge advantage over the other shooters at 300 yards through 1000 yards.

I think you have guessed by now, the material in the last couple of chapters is not directly related to Sight Alignment or Trigger Control. It is, however, of vital importance and needs to be covered. There are hundreds of other things that can affect your accuracy but, unfortunately, I am running out of space. I have tried to stick with my criteria of talking only about things YOU can control. You may need to change your previous methods to achieve this control. To have that control, you must first have the <u>KNOWLEDGE</u>.

FOREWORD

I know it is strange to have a "Foreword" in the middle of a book. I don't consider this the middle, I think of it as an entirely new and different book. It would be too small to stand on its own, so it's tagging along with the rest of this literary endeavor.

Everything you are going to get from here on are my theories, concepts and ideas. You cannot discuss these with someone who hasn't <u>fully</u> read and understood the previous concepts, because they will hear a few key words or phrases and immediately fall back on the old hard line misconceptions that they were taught, and believe. These beliefs are so ingrained; they have the force of "law" and are absolute. Had this been the Dark Ages, I would be tried for heresy for even daring to speak against the "Rule." I may yet find that to be the case. I take encouragement from the few who have discovered, "That's why I have had that problem."

I do want to hear from you. I want your opinion—good or bad. If it is good, I'll know that I'm on the right track. If you disagree, and have **constructive criticisms**, I would like to hear from you. The proof will be in the pudding. Try the system for yourself. Work with it and make up your own mind. You have nothing to lose but your low scores.

I'm going to give you three true stories. The first two will show how the system works.

The last story will show the difficulty of taking a hard and fast "rule," changing it to "a rule of thumb," without everyone thinking you are a High Power "Wacko."

FIRST STORY

Some years ago, I was keeping score for a shooter on the 600-yard line. Something caught my attention on the next firing point. One of our club members, Milt Haggenson, a good old boy, older than dirt, Marksman, was having some difficulty with his string of fire. He was getting complete misses, visible misses, fives, and sixes. He was all over the target.

One week later, we had a 1000-yard team match and I was short one of my shooters. Milt was available and agreed to fill in. During this time, I was working on my theories so I decided to test them. I took away Milt's spotting scope and his scorebook. I plotted his shots and gave him his elevation and windage changes. All he did was shoot. When I had him centered up, I told the scorekeeper he was going for record. The same man (who one week earlier, from 600 yards, could not keep his rounds on paper, and no where near the black) came off the 1000-yard line with seventeen of his twenty rounds in the aiming black. The three shots that were out were within inches of the black at 11 o'clock.

SECOND STORY

Sometime during the mid-1800's, a doctor declared unequivocally, "The normal human body temperature is 98.6 degrees Fahrenheit." When one makes unequivocal pronouncements, with precision to a tenth of a degree, one sounds like one knows what one is talking about. For well over one hundred years, every doctor, nurse, parent, and publication knew the **normal** human body temperature.

Recently, for about three days, all the major TV networks, local stations and newspapers ran a story about the "American Medical Association" announcing the normal human body temperature is not 98.6 degrees. The AMA had determined that "**normal**" was a "range" of temperatures covering a three-degree span; what is "normal" for one person may not be "normal" for another. The news story was reported and soon forgotten. Today, ask any doctor, nurse, and parent, or look in any publication, and they will tell you the "normal" human body temperature is 98.6 degrees! Anything repeated often enough, long enough or loud enough becomes true; even a big lie.

CHAPTER SEVEN

I hadn't known Jack Krieger long before I learned he is an excellent long-range shooter. We were shooting a team match from 1000 yards at Lodi, WI. Jack was shooting and I was coaching. He had fired his first sighter and had a mid-ring nine at nine o'clock. I gave him a windage change of three quarters of a minute right—about one half the usual amount. He looked back at me with a puzzled look; I nodded confirmation, so he did it. His next shot was a dead center X. He laughed and said, "Someday you'll have to tell me how you did that."

One of the first things learned by a new shooter is the "Minute of Angle (MOA) Rule," also known as "The Windage and Elevation Rule":

"One click (Minute) will move the strike of the bullet one inch per hundred yards."

Minute of Angle

• AT	• The Spread Is:
• 100 yds	• 1 inch
• 200 yds	• 2 inches
• 300 yds	• 3 inches
• 600 yds	• 6 inches
• 1,000 yds	• 10 inches

Fig. 68

I'm going to give you an in-depth look at a "Minute of

Angle," where it comes from, how it is used, how it applies to shooting, and how and why the problems occur. Then, I'll give you an alternative "Rule of Thumb" that works far better.

A circle is commonly divided into 360 equal parts known as degrees. Each degree is divided into 60 equal parts, known as "minutes," and each minute is then divided into 60 equal parts, known as "seconds." Navigators, Map Makers and Surveyors, etc. use "Latitude and Longitude," and by using degrees, minutes and seconds, they can pin point any spot on Earth to an accuracy of 101.4333 feet.

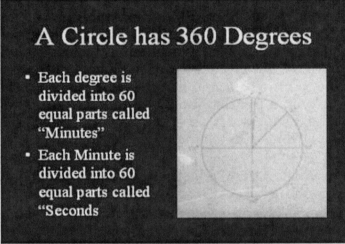

Fig. 69

A MINUTE OF ANGLE

In the construction of an angle, the **apex** is <u>the point where the two legs meet</u>; the spread of these two legs forms the angle. The further from the apex, the wider the spread of the lines (the legs).

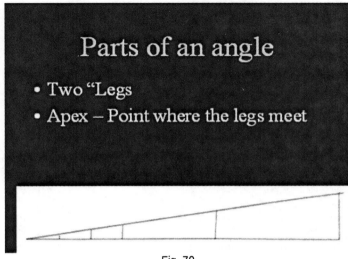

Fig. 70

If the apex of a minute of angle were at the center of the Earth, by the time the lines reached the surface (At the Equator), they would be 6,086 feet apart, or **one nautical mile**. I've learned and have seen in many books that a nautical mile is 6,080 feet. Ron Lamberty is a surveyor and he said it is really 6,086 feet. I'll take his word for it.

IN TERMS OF THE SHOOTING SPORT

Picture the apex at the end of your barrel and the lower line extending straight ahead, off to the horizon. The upper line angles upward and, at given distances, the spread is a given amount at each yard line. Remember, **we are talking about minute of angle**, not degrees or seconds.

For one minute of angle (moa), the spread of the lines at:

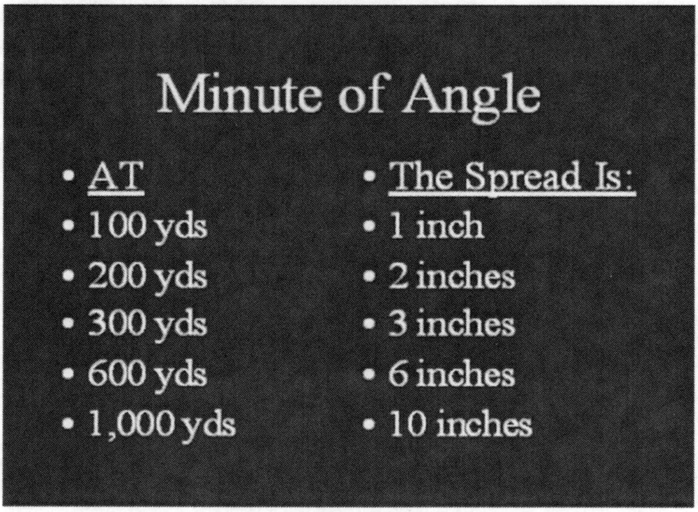

Minute of Angle

• AT	• The Spread Is:
• 100 yds	• 1 inch
• 200 yds	• 2 inches
• 300 yds	• 3 inches
• 600 yds	• 6 inches
• 1,000 yds	• 10 inches

Fig. 71

These are hard and fast scientific facts and no one argues with them. The windage and elevation rule was ADAPTED to fit these hard and fast figures. **A rifle with full minute clicks is said to move the strike of the bullet one inch per hundred yards**. A rifle with 1/2 minute clicks would be 1/2 the rule, a rifle with 1/4 minute clicks would be 1/4 the rule, and a rifle with 1/8 minute clicks would, of course, be 1/8 the rule.

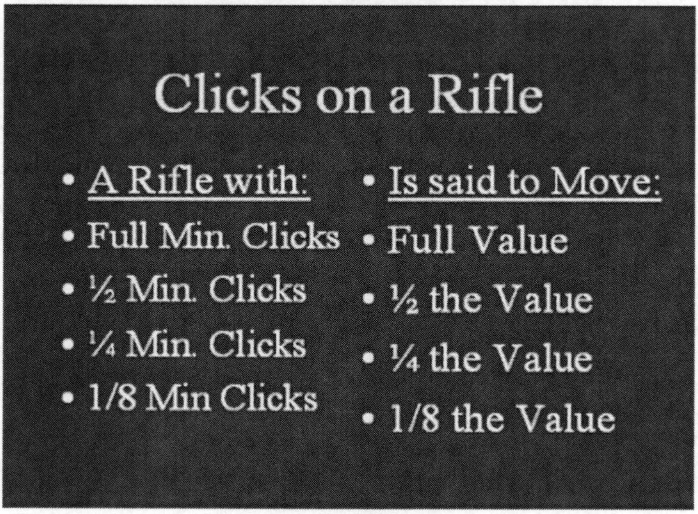

Clicks on a Rifle

• A Rifle with:	• Is said to Move:
• Full Min. Clicks	• Full Value
• ½ Min. Clicks	• ½ the Value
• ¼ Min. Clicks	• ¼ the Value
• 1/8 Min Clicks	• 1/8 the Value

Fig. 72

This is a rule with which you must do two things:

(1) MEMORIZE IT
Because people will talk about it

(2) FORGET IT
IT DOES <u>NOT</u> WORK

The makers of the score book (it is <u>not</u> a score book, it is a DATA book, It contains a lot more information than your scores) provide a great service, along with a dis-service to the shooting community. Each maker of a data book tries to make his a little better than the others, and makes room for more and more data; I won't go into all the features at this time. The dis-service is that they **all repeat the big lie—The grid lines printed over the picture of the target are in minutes**, based on the <u>Golden</u> Rule of Shooting, The Windage and Elevation Rule.

The aiming black and all the scoring rings on each target have set dimensions for their diameter. They can be found in the NRA High Power Rule Book. To do your calculations, you have to change the diameter dimensions to radius dimensions, or 1/2 the given scoring ring. **We use the radius because it goes to the center of the target and that is where we want our shots**.

You cannot blame the makers of the data books. Logically, if the shot is on the target a given number of inches from the center, and you know the sizes of the scoring rings, you should be able to overlay some grid lines (based on the windage and elevation rule) onto the target to aid in determining the number of clicks to move your sights, to center your next shot.

Fig. 73

The new shooter will use these grid lines; he trusts them because they are **based on the "Rule**," which is based on hard scientific facts (when one quotes down to tenths of degrees in temperature, within inches at hundreds of yards, it makes one sound like he knows what he is talking about). When the shooter uses the grid lines the trouble begins; he will overcompensate and his shot will go out the other side of the black (or at least outside the ten ring).

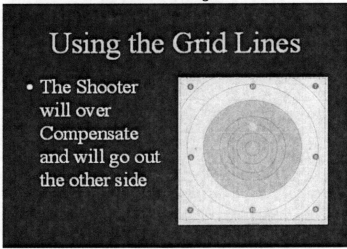

Fig. 74

Someone will say, "You must have put one click on the rifle and one click in your head!" The shooter believes the grid lines are right and the "Rule" is correct so, he thinks; "It must be me. Maybe I did put one click on the rifle and one click in my head." I have heard that statement hundreds of times, but I have never heard anyone explain how to prevent or stop it.

Sages say that it is good for one to act foolishly on occasion. At the risk of looking foolish, I will be the one to tell you how to prevent the dreaded "one click on the rifle and one click in the head" syndrome.

If the Windage and Elevation rule a.k.a. (Also Known As) the Minute of Angle (MOA) rule does not work, then, what does work?

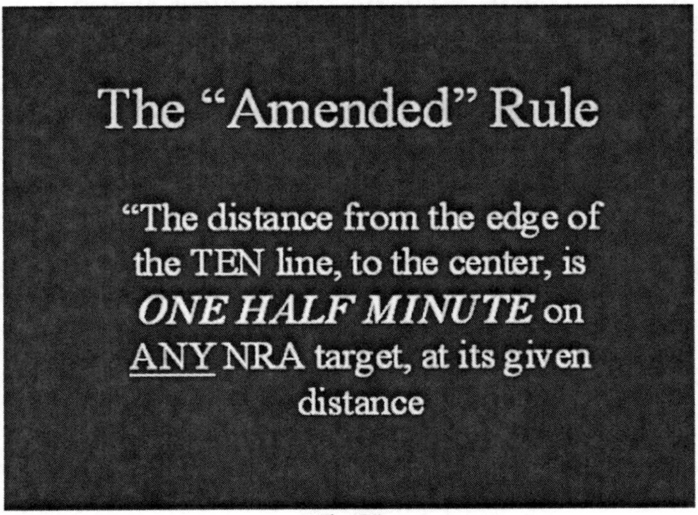

The "Amended" Rule

"The distance from the edge of the TEN line, to the center, is *ONE HALF MINUTE* on ANY NRA target, at its given distance

Fig. 75

From 30+ years of personal experience and the observation of other shooters, I developed what I call the "Amended Rule." The distance from the edge of the 10 line, to the center of the target, is **one half minute** on any NRA target, at its given distance.

When I say "Any NRA target at its given distance," I mean you cannot take a 600 yard target and shoot at it from 200

105

yards and expect the amended rule to work. Or take a 200 yard target and shoot it from 600 yards and expected it to work.

The amended rule first came to my mind when shooting sighter shots for 300 yard rapid fire, using my Winchester model 70, bolt gun, I noticed on several occasions when I had a shot on the 10 line at 3 o'clock, I would use 1/2 minute left windage and the next sighter would be a dead center X. That got me thinking.

Before I get started there are two assumptions that must be made. They are the same assumptions that are made for the windage and elevation rule. **First, the rifle must be in good mechanical working order**. Appendix A shows a list of possible problems and any one of them can cause a loss of accuracy. The amended rule, or the rule itself, cannot work if your rifle has a loose gas cylinder plug, a sticking gas piston, or a broken hand guard. Your accuracy is zilch, and <u>any</u> rule or rule of thumb will not help.

The second assumption is that your sight alignment, trigger control, and, particularly, your focus, are all correct. If you are doing something wrong and are trying to make sight adjustments based on the Rule of Thumb (or the rule), it will not work. (You will think that I'm "some kind of nut" and there are already enough people around who are willing to agree).

NOTE: Before anyone says anything about service rifle, bolt rifle, half minute sights, quarter minute sights, eighth minute sights, different sight radius, or calibers and weights of bullets, I want to say: from shooting and coaching, I have found this theory or rule of thumb works the same on <u>all</u> the elements mentioned above. The "Rule" is assumed to work under all these different conditions, and no one tries to introduce these variables.

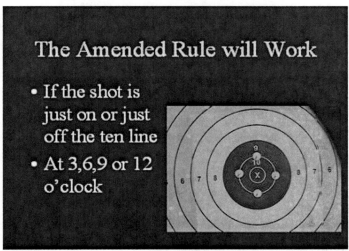

Fig. 76

I'm going to give you three examples, one for each yard line (200, 300 & 600).

Fig. 77

I'll give you the dimensions of the ten ring, look at the "Rule", and then tell you what the amended rule would be. I'm going to keep these examples very simple. I want you to understand this and I want you to <u>remember</u> it for the rest of your life. In these three examples resides the key to the whole theory. The examples are simple, but effective.

In the first example, a shot is on the ten line at six o'clock

(Figure 78) on a 200 yard target. The ten ring on this target is seven inches in diameter or three and one half inches from the outer edge to the center. According to the "Rule", you would move your sights <u>one and three quarter minutes</u>.

Figure 78
A 200 yard target with a "spotter in the 10-ring" at six o'clock.

I guarantee if you come up 1-3/4 minutes, you <u>will</u> go out the top of the ten ring (and maybe even the black).

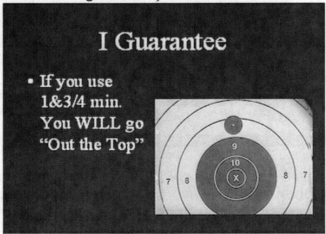

Fig. 79

Your shooting partner will say, "You must have put one click on the rifle and one click in your head."

WHAT YOU SHOULD DO

Come up **one half minute!!!** Yes, 1/2 minute will center your shot and you will not go out the other side. If your shot is just in or just out of the ten line, or right on it, use 1/2 minute for a correction.

The 1/2-minute you should use is almost one third of the "Rule".

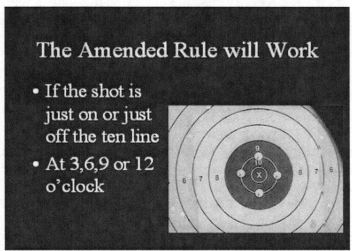

Fig. 80

Like the rule, this works for both elevation and windage and in each direction.

In the second example, on the 300-yard target, the shot is again on the ten line at six o'clock and, again, the ten ring is seven inches in diameter and the distance to the center is three and one half inches.

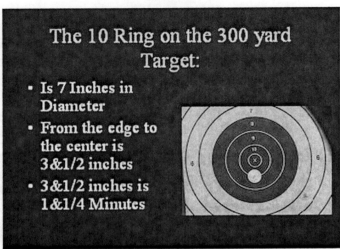

Fig. 81

The "Rule" says you should use <u>one and one-quarter minutes</u>, which is really 3.75 inches or just over half way. Again, I guarantee, if you use one and one-quarter minutes at 300 yards, you will go out the top. With a ten on the line or very near it, move the sights **One Half Minute** at 300 yards. This time the amount is almost 1/2 the "Rule."

The last example is the 600-yard target and, again, the shot is on the ten line at six o'clock. The ten ring on the 600 yard target is twelve inches in diameter or six inches from the outer edge to the center. Six inches at 600 yards is one minute, the amount the "Rule" says you should come up in this example.

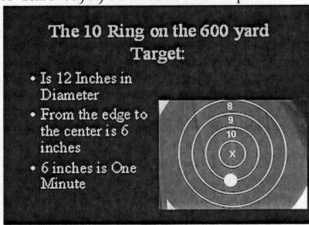

Fig. 82

If you come up one full minute in this situation, you may get lucky and still catch a ten, <u>at twelve o'clock</u>. From 600 yards and with a shot on or near the ten line, move the sights **One Half Minute!!!** This time the amount is one half the "Rule." Look at the "Amended Rule" as being fluid, one third to one half the "Rule." The Amended Rule is a "Rule of Thumb" and not a hard and fast figure.

Jerry VanTreeck is a fine, young, former Marine, and a High Power shooter and had just become Distinguished. I was pulling targets for Jerry while he shot a 600-yard practice string when he had a shot just off the ten line at six o'clock. He fired again and had another hit, right next to the last shot, and was still just off the ten line. Jerry's next shot was just off the ten line at twelve o'clock. I immediately knew how much elevation he used and what he should have used. When I asked him, he confirmed that he had used one *full minute* change. After he had gone out the top, he came back down *one half minute.*

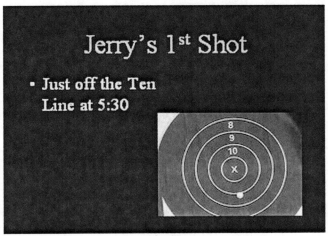

Fig. 83

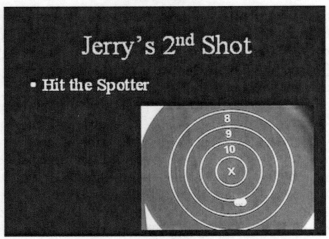
Fig. 84

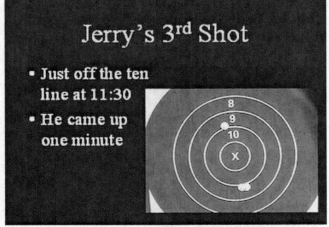
Fig. 85

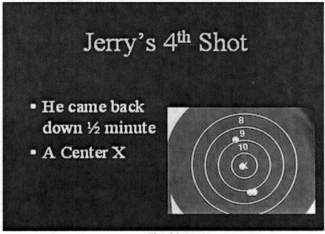

Fig. 86

THE KEY

The key to the "Amended Rule" is:

"The distance from the edge of the <u>TEN</u> line, to the center, on *ANY* NRA target, is ONE HALF MINUTE at its given distance."

Again

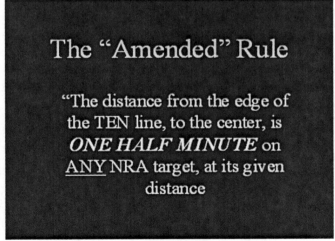

Fig. 87

This works on the 200, 300, 600, 800, 900 and 1,000 yard targets at their respective ranges. For the reduced targets SR-42 and the MR52, for the National Match Course at 200 yards you will find the system works the same.

Again

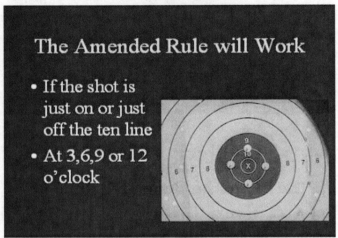

Fig. 88

My Personal Experience

I was shooting and NRA National Match (reduced, 200 yards) Course. The National Match Course is 10 shot standing (slow fire), 10 shots sitting rapid, 10 shots prone rapid and 20 shots 600 yards (slow fire).

The 300 yard rapid fire for reduced 200 yards uses the MR-42 target to simulate the 300 yards. We had sighter shots at each stage of fire.

I shot of score of 100 with 10Xs. Generally that is a "Once in a lifetime achievement." It goes right along with my "Other once in a lifetime achievement"—I had a "Hole in One" playing golf.

The groups shown in Figures 89 and 90. The two pasters shown was the two sighter shots. A point halfway between the two sighters and the distance to the center of the target measured __One-Inch__.

Since I am firing from 200 yards, the "Rule" says I should come down 1/2 minute. I knew better, and I used my "__Amended Rule__" and I came down 1/4 minute and as you can see I almost lost some shots out the bottom of the x-ring. In fact, had I come down the 1/2 minute the Rule called for, I would have lost a lot more of the Xs. The nice thing about the Amended Rule is it will also work on reduce course targets, as long as they are made to be shot at that particular distance.

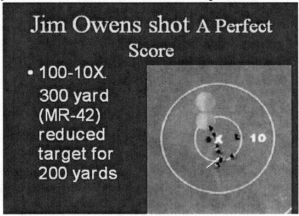

Fig. 89

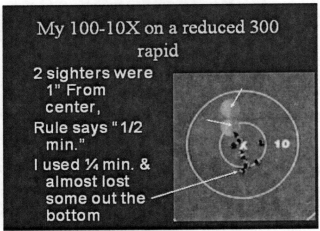

My 100-10X on a reduced 300 rapid

2 sighters were 1" From center,
Rule says "1/2 min."
I used ¼ min. & almost lost some out the bottom

Fig. 90

Now that you have the key to the system, you simply make your adjustments based on the "Amended Rule." If the distance from the center to the outer edge of the ten line is one half minute, then one half that distance is one quarter of a minute change on the sights.

If you have a shot further out, just take the distance from the center to the edge of the ten line and double it to get one full minute. If your shot is between there and the ten line, use three quarters of a minute sight change to center up.

I talked to many High-Master shooters and several National Champions and they agree the amended rule works. I have had literally hundreds of people tell me "Thank you, this has helped me shoot better." I also have had 5 or 6 people tell me "You are full of $ _ _ T, it does not work." No one said you have to use it, but give it a try, you may like it.

For your convenience, you will find in Appendix C, pictures of the 200, 300, 600, and 1000-yard targets, with the old grid lines removed and new grid lines based on the "Amended Rule."

The "Jim Owens Data Book" has the "Amended" grid lines on each page. Also some features included are; A chart for "Normal Come ups", A chart for rapid fire problems, a range check-list, Wind Charts, A wind speed estimating guide, some "Round Count" pages and more.

Fig. 91

The Data Book can be ordered from my web site: www.JarHeadTop.com

This chapter covered the <u>FIRST HALF</u> of my theory. It will stand-alone. You can use it without employing the second half, and it will help you center your shots faster and keep you from going out the other side as often as you have in the past. The next chapter will cover another theory. When combined with this chapter, it will show you a whole new way of looking at the shooting sport.

CHAPTER EIGHT

The term "Minute of Angle" also known as MOA is a generic term, as far as the shooting community is concerned. It is a scientific term and was adapted to fit the Windage and Elevation rule as discussed in the last chapter.

Minute of Angle is also used to describe a "group" size, i.e., one minute of angle, two minutes of angle, three minutes of angle or larger. An example: a string of fire from 300 yards, grouping three inches or less, would be a minute of angle group, or "within" a minute. A six-inch group at 300 yards is said to be a two-minute group.

I have heard people say, "You <u>must</u> shoot within a minute of angle to shoot well." **That is two inches or less at 200 yards,** three inches or less at 300 yards, and six inches or less at 600 yards. The person who could do that would <u>never</u> be beaten. It is a great aspiration and one that can be achieved, but not on a regular basis. At any yard line, a centered group within a minute of angle is a score of 100 with ten Xs.

A three hundred game in bowling is far more common than a 100 with ten Xs in shooting. In twenty-eight years of shooting, I have seen only six perfect scores. Three were on the Marine Corps team. Boots Obermeyer had one from 300 yards on a Wednesday night practice (Fig. 92).

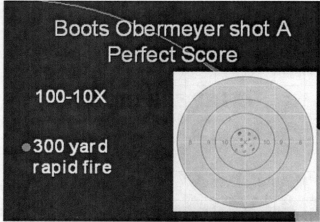

Fig. 92

I had one on the SR-42 target (reduced 300 yards); fired at 200 yards, in a league match (Fig. 93).

Fig. 93

Credit has to be given where credit is due. Boots' son, Eric Obermeyer, fired Slow Fire Prone from the 200-yard line on the MR-52 target (reduced 600), and had a score of 200 - 20X (Fig. 94). I measured the X ring and looked it up in the rulebook. It is 1.79 inches. That is within the minute of angle. That summer, Eric also had scores of 200 - 15X and 200 - 17X.

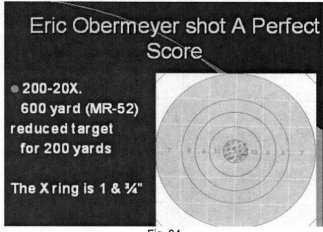

Fig. 94

As nice as they are, 100-10X scores are few and far between, if ever! The accepted reality is: even High Masters seldom shoot minute of angle groups. You can shoot two or three minute groups and still achieve High Master scores (Fig. 96).

Fig. 95

The ten-ring at 600 yards is twelve inches. That is two minutes of angle. Keep the group centered and you have a score of 200, Fig 97. Later, I'll show how a three-minute group of 18 inches will still get you a High Master score.

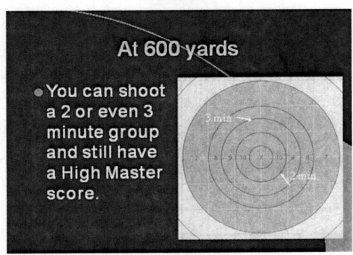

Fig. 96

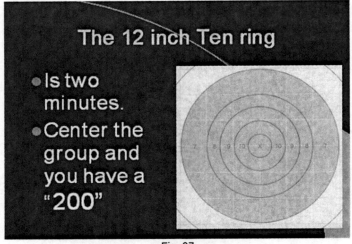

Fig. 97

AWARENESS AND THE ABSTRACT CONCEPT

Trying to explain a theory is like running a railroad. First, you want to make sure everyone is on board and understands where you are going. You start out slow and gain momentum. When you come up to speed, and make the trip by explaining the theory, you hope you haven't lost anyone along the way.

The first step is awareness. Have you ever driven past a certain building or other object hundreds of times and never noticed it? Someone points out the object and you now notice it for the first time; it has entered your consciousness. You say to yourself, "Wow, when did they put that there?" You know it wasn't there yesterday! From that point on, you will always notice it, same thing with a make of car. You just got one, and you now notice there are lots of others just like it on the road. They all suddenly appeared, they entered your consciousness, and you became aware of them.

The next step is to make sure everyone knows or remembers what an abstract concept is. Something abstract is something that cannot be seen, heard, felt, smelled or tasted. It is an idea or theory. I guess that alone makes it abstract. A few examples are: time travel, Darwin's theory, perpetual motion, and nuclear fission.

The one I think comes closest to what I have in mind is the Human Aura. I suppose the best way to describe it is as an invisible glow around the human body. In fact, all living things have an aura. I saw a special on the *Discovery Channel* some years ago. They were showing Kirilian Photography; looks like an x-Ray. They could photograph the human aura; it cannot be seen by the physical eye, but it is there. They also did a leaf, and the aura even remains for a short time after part of the leaf is gone. They cut the leaf in half and photographed it again. You could see the half of the leaf, but the full aura was still there. The half that had been cut was already starting to fade.

For you younger people, think of this as an image on a computer screen. You can turn the image, change its shape

123

and enlarge it. I'm going to give you an image to do just that, with your imagination. We will then apply it to shooting.

When a person says, "That gun is a one holer!" (Fig. 98) we all know that it is just an expression to mean the rifle shoots really well. There was something about the phrase that bothered me. As I thought about it, I realized the following: If it did shoot through the same hole each time, it would shoot the spotter out twenty-one times. Due to the safety factor, and the shortage of spindles, I'm glad that is not the case. So, what is the case?

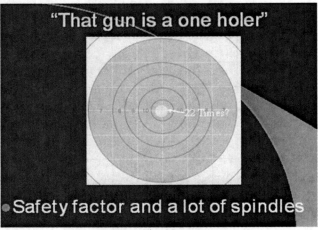

Fig. 98

Fig. 99

124

Picture a DIXIE® cup shaped like a cone. We are going to take the DIXIE® cup, and turn it, change its shape, and enlarge it. First, lay the opening of the cone down onto a piece of paper, with the point straight up. Take a pencil and draw around the outer edge. Lift the cup and you have a circle (Fig. 101). In the exact center of the circle, place a small cross (+).

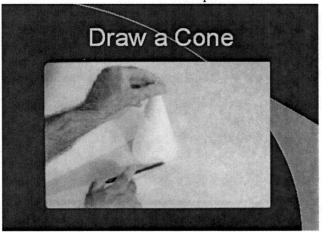

Fig. 100

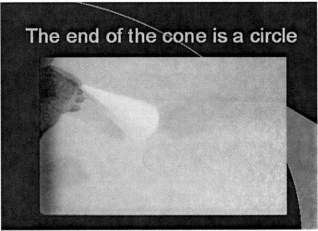

Fig. 101

125

Still using your imagination, take a pair of scissors and snip off the tip of the cone, and place the cone over the end of your muzzle. Now, <u>elongate</u> it until it reaches, from your rifle on the 600-yard line at (the tip of the cone), to the target (the opening of the cone). Now push the computer button in your imagination and the cone fades from sight. Only you can see it.

Fig. 102

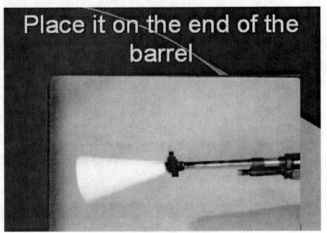

Fig. 103

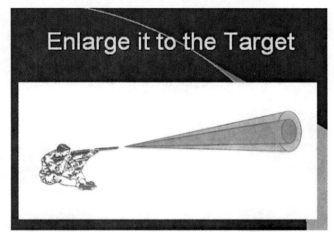

Fig. 104

Fig. 105

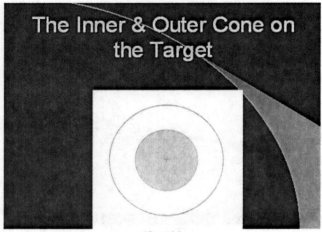

Fig. 106

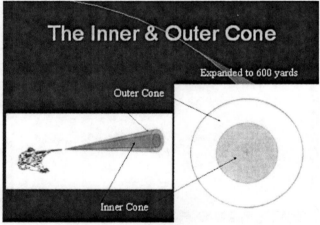

Fig. 107

As you fire each shot (WITHOUT MOVING THE SIGHTS OR A WIND CHANGE), **<u>Your shots will pattern in the conical shape and will fall within a circular pattern on the target</u>**. The small cross (+) is at the center of that pattern (No matter where your sights are set, as long as you are on the target). Granted, due to the wind, your pattern will be more like an ellipse. To keep this as simple as possible, assume we are in a no wind condition.

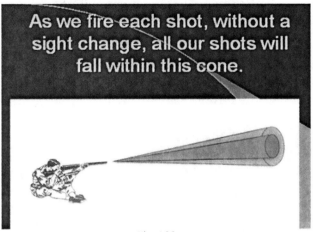

Fig. 108

The size of the circular pattern or cone will increase or decrease, (larger or smaller groups), based on a number of factors: the mechanical working order of the rifle (See Appendix A), the quality of your ammunition, the equipment you use, your knowledge, your position, and your ability. If you have a mechanical problem (say, a loose gas piston plug), your group or cone **will** grow larger, due to the fliers. All the ability in the world will not help until the problem is located and corrected. Once corrected, your group size grows smaller, and so does your cone.

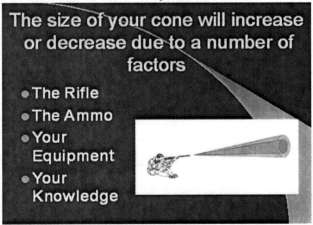

Fig. 109

Now that you have this 600-yard invisible cone from your rifle to the target, let's get a little stranger. We are going to add a second smaller cone, within the first cone, in our computer image. They both start at the muzzle of your rifle, and both reach the target in a circular pattern, and they both have the same center (+). If I have lost anyone up to this point, see Figure 105 to help you picture this concept. Think of this as the aura of your bullet flight. No one can see it, feel it, or touch it, but you are now aware that it is there. Whether you read on and make the most use of it is up to you. Even if you ignore it, the aura is still there.

1. Dispersion of the Shots within the Cones

<u>Approximately 55-60% of your shots will be within the inner cone</u> (HOLD IT—where did you get these figures?). PAUSE. These figures are based on three things: (1) observation and study; (2) talking with National and State Champions; (3) it's my theory, and I'll assign any damn numbers I want. Do you have a problem with that? (NO—ok, just asking).

<u>Approximately 55-60% of your shots will be within this inner cone. About 20% of your shots will be *just outside* the inner cone. The remaining shots will be part of the Standard Deviation or "Wild Shot Fairies."</u> To quote an American Indian Shaman, "Sometimes the magic works, sometimes it doesn't."

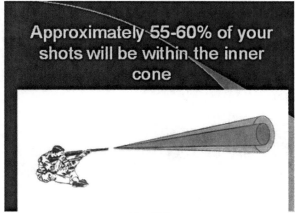

Fig. 110

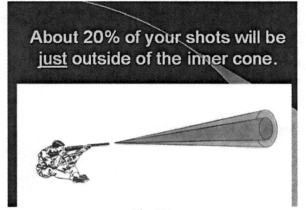

Fig. 111

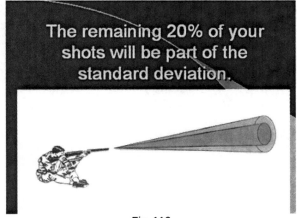

Fig. 112

Let's say you are shooting 600 yards and the size of your cone is 18 inches or three minutes of angle.

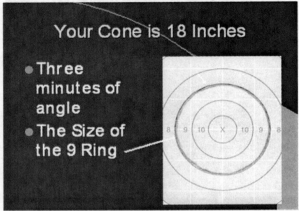

Fig.113

When the center of your cone's (+) is placed over the center of the target (the X ring), you have the correct zero on your rifle and the correct wind setting. No matter what windage and elevation you have on the rifle **ALL YOUR SHOTS WILL FALL WITHIN YOUR CONE**.

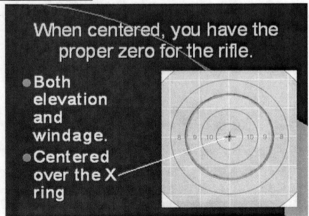

Fig. 114

Your inner cone is 60% of your overall 18-inch cone or 10.8 inches.

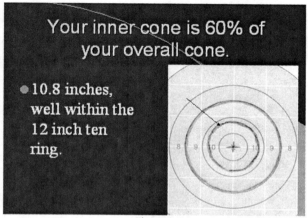

Fig. 115

This is well within the 12 inch ten-ring. 60% of your 20 rounds is 12 shots, which is within the ten-ring.

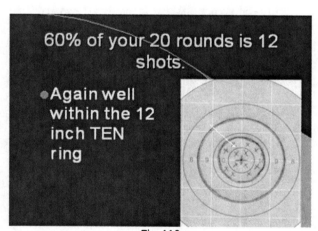

Fig. 116

The remaining 1 1/4 of the ten ring will take at least another 10%, or two rounds, even if they are just touching the ten line.

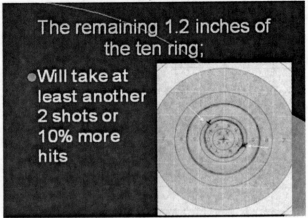

Fig. 117

Another 10% will be just off the ten line giving you two close nines.

The remaining 20% will be part of your standard deviation in the outer edge of your 18 inch overall cone. This will give you four wide nines.

Fig. 118

You have just shot a High Master score, 194, with three minutes of angle hold. To achieve this you must:

1. Center the cone.

2. Keep track of the wind.

3. Align the sights and squeeze the trigger.

4. Do not muscle the rifle.

WHEN YOU MOVE YOUR SIGHTS, YOU ARE NOT MOVING A PARTICULAR SHOT. YOU ARE MOVING THE CENTER OF YOUR CONE (+)

Fig. 119

Any time you move your sights, you are **NOT** moving a single shot, you are moving your cone and <u>ALL YOUR SHOTS WILL FALL WITHIN YOUR CONE</u>.

A whole new way of looking at shooting

Remember that time you had a hit on the target, came two clicks left, and the next shot was in the same spot? Look at it this way: the first shot was at <u>nine o'clock in your outer cone.</u> When you came two clicks left, you moved the center of your cone to the left, either *onto* the spotter or *past it*. Now your next shot was either within your inner cone, if you moved onto the spotter, or the shot could be <u>at three o'clock</u> of your outer cone, if you had moved past the spotter. In either case, the second shot would come up in the same spot.

It gives you a whole new way of looking at shooting—DOESNT IT?

Fig. 121

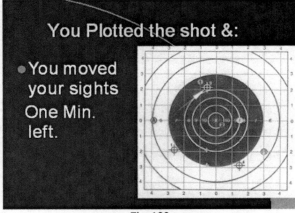

Fig. 122

Fig. 123

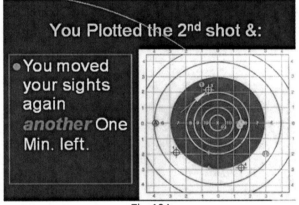

Fig. 124

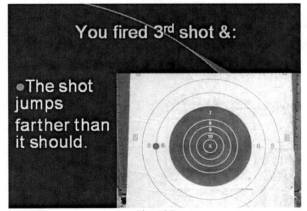

Fig. 125

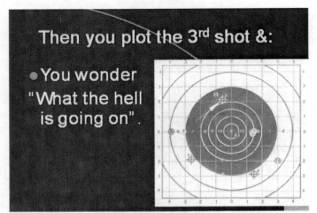

Fig. 126

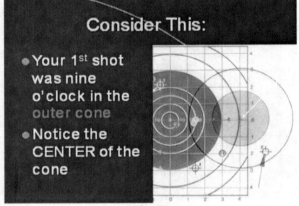

Fig.127

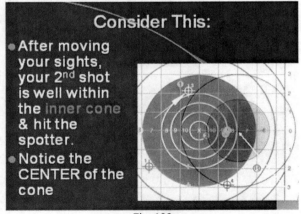

Fig. 128

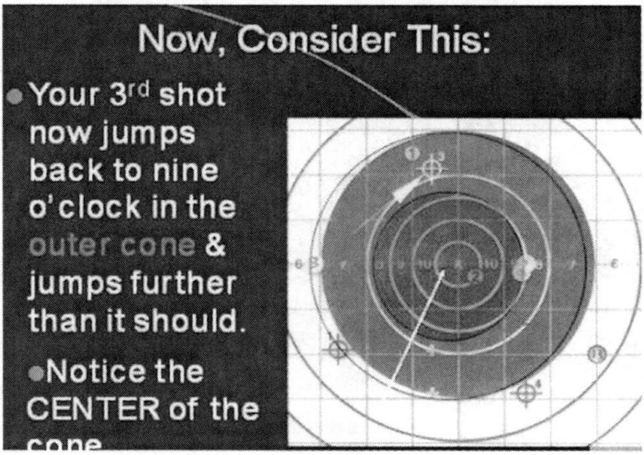

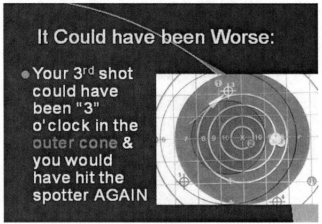

Now, Consider This:

- Your 3rd shot now jumps back to nine o'clock in the outer cone & jumps further than it should.
- Notice the CENTER of the cone.

Fig. 129

It Could have been Worse:

- Your 3rd shot could have been "3" o'clock in the outer cone & you would have hit the spotter AGAIN

Fig. 130

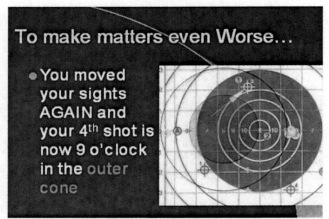

Fig 131

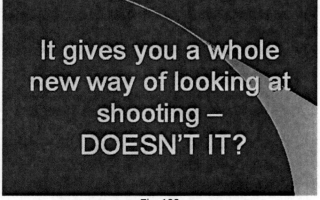

Fig. 132

CHAPTER NINE

This chapter, I thought, was going to be extremely difficult to explain. I was afraid I would lose you in the attempt. In the class, I use a great number of colored slides as visual aids. Here, I do not have that luxury. I settled on a couple of figures with a group of different markings. Each one is explained in the text. To insure my accuracy, I made a simple aid to check each step. It worked so well I would like you to make one and follow along as I explain the text. A sample gauge is provided in Appendix D, however it is better to make your own. I was amazed at how much it helped to focus the concept of the "Amended Rule".

To make your own gauge, take a 3 x 5 card or any piece of scrap paper, and make a simple marking gauge (See Fig. 133). You have to use the 600-yard page from your scorebook (NOTE: Be careful, not all books have the scoring rings proportional. At that time I used the "Creedmoor Data Book.) As a reminder, my Data Book has all the pages with the grid lines for the "Amended Rule."

Lay the card onto the 600-yard page, placing the upper left corner of the card on the center of the target— X-ring. Using the vertical and horizontal grid lines, keep the card straight. With the left corner on the center of the X, mark a short line on the card, even with the **ten** line at three o'clock. Label this line "1/2." Make a longer line even with the **eight-ring** and label it "1." Move this last line to the left until it is on the center of the X, making sure the card stays horizontal. Make another short mark, again at the ten line, and label it "1 1/2." Mark the longer line at the eight-ring and label it "**2**." Again, shift this line to the center and mark the "2 1/2" and "3" lines in the same manner.

Repeat the process once more for the "3 1/ 2" and "4" lines. *Your point of reference is the line of the ten-ring as 1/2 minute for the amended rule.*

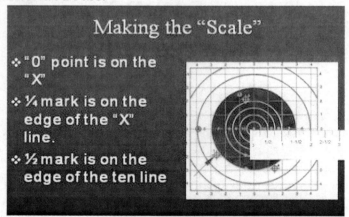

Fig. 133

For you bolt rifle shooters with 1/4-minute sights, you may notice, that on this **Target (600 yard) only**, the X-line is one-quarter minute. The nine- line is three-quarter minutes. The eight-line is one full minute and the distance from the eight -line to the edge of the black is one-half minute. The seven, six, and five-rings are twice the size of the inner ones. See Fig. 134

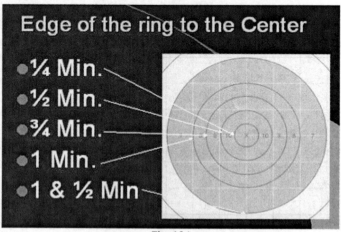

Fig. 134

I want to give you an example of what typically happens with a new shooter and what can be accomplished using the amended rule and centering the cone.

This "<u>Theory</u>" is based on my observation of one of our shooters <u>firing slow fire at 600 yards</u>. He was all over the target and had five, sixes, visible misses and complete misses.

Fig. 135

One week later I coached him at 1,000 yards and he shoot 17 out of 20 shots "In the aiming black." The three shots that were out of the bull's eye were "Just out at 11 o'clock."

So...

We have a Marksman with a six-minute of angle hold. Six minutes is 36 inches at 600 yards, the same size as the aiming black. See Fig. 136

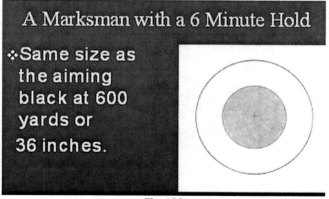

Fig. 136

For a Quick Review – Remember

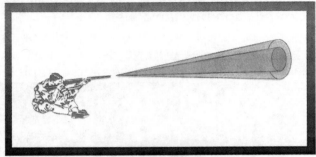

Fig. 137
You have two cones inside the other

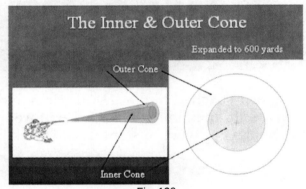

Fig. 138
The dark shading is the inner cone

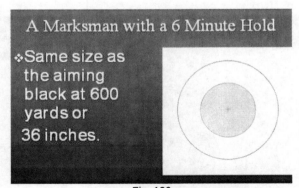

Fig. 139
A six minute hold is the size of the 600 yd. Aiming black

Note: The two circles in Fig. 139 is also known as "The Overlay" when it is placed on the target. This represents his cone both inner (Dark) and outer (White). <u>The little + in the center of his cone is his "Sight Setting"</u> or better known as his "Windage and Elevation" settings or sometimes called his "Dope." Remember **ALL SHOTS WILL FALL WHITHIN THIS CONE, EVEN IF IT IS NOT CENERED OVER THE BULLS EYE.**

Fig. 140

The most important thing to remember is <u>**ANY TIME YOU MOVE YOUR SIGHTS (Windage or Elevation) YOU ARE NOT MOVING A SINGLE SHOT — YOU ARE MOVING YOUR ENTIRE CONE!!!**</u>

Let's get Started

Our Marksman does not know that he has a six-minute hold or that he has a cone, or the ways to reduce its size, or that he has the proper method to center his group. He does not know of the "amended minute of angle rule." He takes "the Rule" as gospel. He believes in the grid lines in his scorebook. He is a graduate of the **"Let's chase the spotter"** school of shooting.

An example of a shot string where the shooter used the Traditional "minute of angel" rule.

Let's take a typical 600-yard string for our aspiring Marksman. He has never kept up his data book. He does not know his zero. We are going to put his zero, the center of his cone, at eight o'clock, just out of the black. (See Figure 141). This is marked 1+. That is his first sight setting and our starting point.

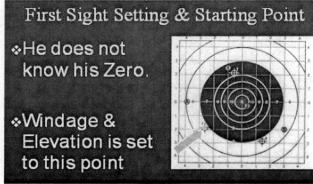

Fig. 141
He takes his first sighter and it is a wide six at nine o'clock.

Fig. 142

It is marked with an "A." in his data book.*

* NOTE: I have a preferred method of marking the shots in my data book. I always mark the 1st sighter with an "A" and I mark the 2nd sighter with a "B." This keeps the sighter shots separate from the numbers. For the 1st ten shots I like to use **small** numbers; 1,2,3,4,5,6,7,8,9,10. For the second ten shots I again use small numbers, but each one has a circle around it. The eleventh shot would be a small 1 with a circle around it and so on for the rest of the string of fire. If you are at long range and are pounding tens and Xs, the center soon becomes a big blob. You simply look at the ones outside the blob and "Be Happy."

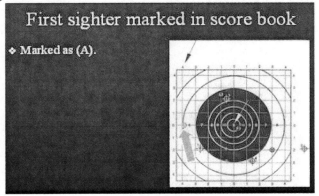

Fig. 143

Using your imaginary circle or cone, with the center at 1+, "A" is in his outer cone at about ten o'clock.

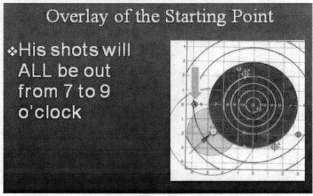

Fig. 144

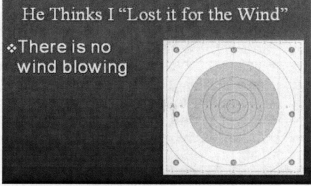

Fig. 145

He thinks, "I'm good for elevation, but I lost it for wind."

Our shooter looks at the grid lines in his score book and they tell him four minutes right.

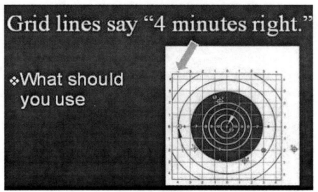

Fig. 146

Take your marking gauge and place the upper left hand corner on the "A." TWO minutes right would have been more appropriate.

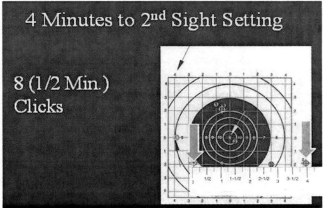

Fig. 147

Our shooter moves his sights four minutes to the right. Remember, he is moving the center of his cone (or zero) four minutes right, not just the nine o'clock shot. Because of the inaccuracy of the "Rule," **he has just over–compensated**, moving the center of his cone to outside the scoring rings, just off the five line at four o'clock. Place your marking gauge on 1+ and read four minutes and you should get 2+, <u>his second sight setting</u>.

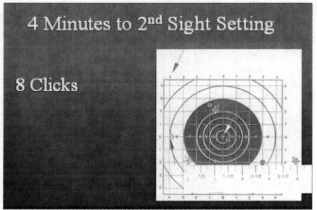

Fig. 148

Many of his problems can be shown at this point.
Imagine his 36-inch circle with the center at 2+. If his next
shot should be at three o'clock, on the outer edge, he will
completely miss the target, off the right hand side.

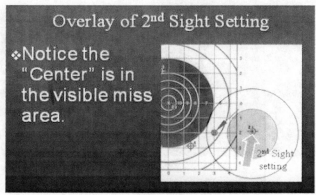

Fig. 149

Fig. 150

Even if his next shot is near the center of his cone, he will have a visible miss at four o'clock, just out of the scoring rings. We will be good to him and place his shot at nine o'clock in his cone. He has a six at four o'clock, marked a "B."

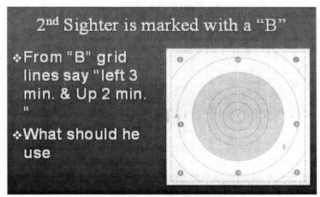

Fig. 151

The grid lines tell him he should come up two minutes and left three minutes. Use your marking gauge and see what you should do. I get <u>one</u> minute up and <u>one and one half</u> minute left. **Remember, you are taking this reading off his spotter "B", not his zero 2+.**

The shooter moves his sights left three minutes. Let's see what this does to his zero. Place your marking gauge on 2+. It should come to a little tick mark just outside the eight ring at about 6:30.

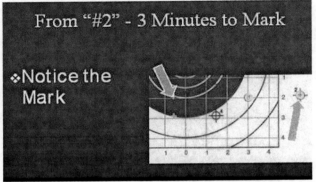

Fig. 152

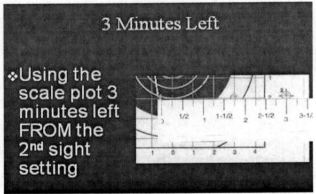

Fig. 153

Now use your gauge to come up two full minutes. His new sight setting is marked 3+.

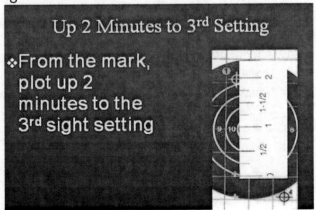

Fig. 154

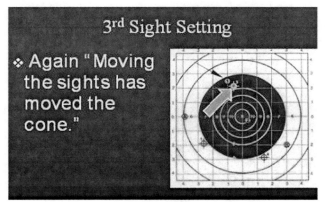

Fig. 155

Fig. 156

His first shot for record is very close to the center of his cone, and is marked with a number one, inside a small circle.

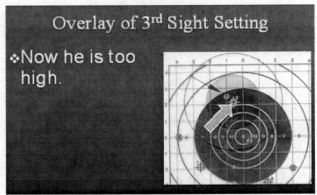

Fig. 157

Fig.158

Our shooter again looks at the grid lines and from his spotter; they tell him to come down 2 1/2 minutes and right one minute. Use your gauge; one half right would be better, and he should come down 1 1/4. If he has only half-minute sights, one full minute (or one and one half) would be far better than the 2 1/2 he used. Remember to take the reading off of his spotter (the number one inside the small circle), and not the 3+.

For the third time, he moves his sights and over compensates. He comes down two and one half minutes and right one full minute. From the center of his cone (3+), use the gauge and come down 2 1/2 minutes. You should come to a second tick mark. From that mark go one full minute right to 4+.

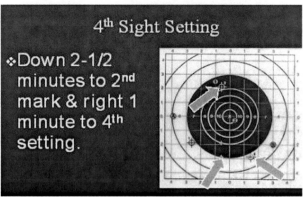

Fig. 159

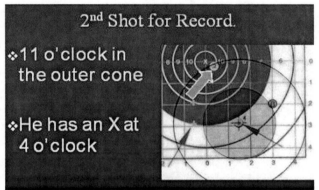

Fig. 160

He takes his second shot for record. It is at eleven o'clock in his cone, and it catches an X, on the line, at four o'clock (Marked with a number two inside a small circle). He says, "Hot Dog! I've got it now." **I'll leave it to your imagination what the rest of his string will be like.**

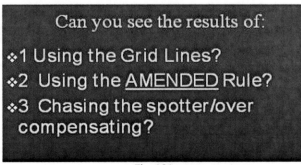

Fig. 161

THE CORRECT WAY
(This is the method I used when coaching him at 1,000 yards)

His friend, another Marksman has had some training and he now knows a few things: he knows that he has a cone, he knows of the amended rule and he knows of the system to correctly use the two. I will again give an example of a typical string of fire, from 600 yards, using the marking gauge.

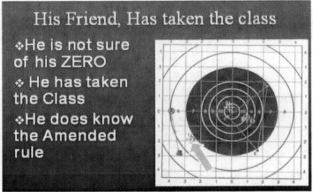

His Friend, Has taken the class

- He is not sure of his ZERO
- He has taken the Class
- He does know the Amended rule

Fig. 162

Our shooter has a six-minute cone, 36 inches, the size of the 600-yard aiming black. (NOTE: This time, our shooter will have quarter minute sights for illustration purposes).

He knows that he wants to center his cone in the black. He also knows that when he moves his sights, he is moving the center of his cone (or zero)—not each shot. He knows he will be patterning his shots in an area that will take up the entire black. He also knows that moving his sights after every shot can cause problems.

Starting the center of the shooter's cone just out of the black at eight o'clock. (See Figure 163).

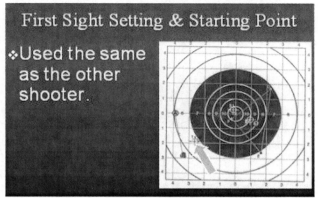

Fig. 163

We will place his first sighter in the same spot, a wide six at nine o'clock, again marked with an "A."

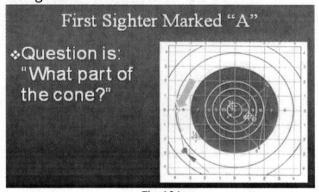

Fig. 164

Let's start his string of fire. He takes his first sighter, and it comes up a wide six at nine o'clock. He marks it in his data book with an "A." Let's turn on our imaginary computer and look at the potential problems. Figure 165 shows this shot (intended to go into the X-ring) to be within four possible cones other than the center of his intended X-ring cone. Is the shot at three o'clock, as in cone A? At nine o'clock, as in cone B? Possibly six o'clock, as in Cone C? Perhaps, it is at twelve o'clock, as in Cone D. Another possibility exists. It could be dead center of his cone. **He needs more information**.

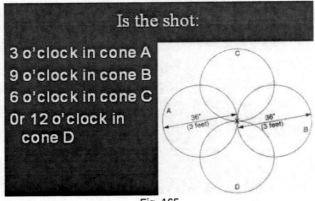

Fig. 165

Four possible cones where the shot could fall.

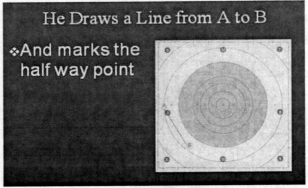

Fig. 166

<u>Without moving his sights</u>, he takes his second sighter. It comes up a five at about seven or seven-thirty. He marks this shot with a "B."

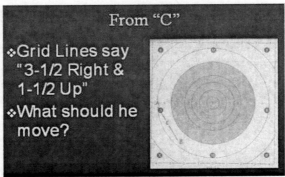

Fig. 167

The ideal situation would be to take a third sighter, form a triangle, and move the sights, based on the center of that triangle. However, he only has two sighter shoots, so he draws a line from "A" to "B" and, at the midway point; he makes a mark and labels it "C."

Now, based on the amended rule, he makes a sight adjustment. The grid lines tell him he should move his sights 3 1/2 minutes right and 1 1/2 minutes up. He knows that is too much.

With some experience, the working gauge will be in your head, but for now, use the gauge. You will see that, from "C," the sights should come 1 3/4 minutes right and just 3/4 of a minute up. He makes this change. Let's see what that does to the center of his cone.

From 1+ (his starting point, remember), measure 1&3/4 right and 3/4 of a minute up.

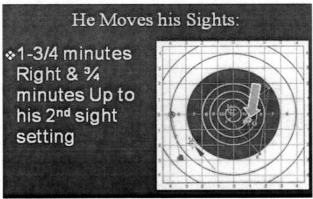

Fig. 168

His zero is now at 2+, which is a ten at four o'clock, a lot better than a visible miss at four o'clock.

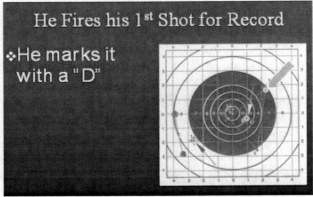

Fig. 169

Our shooter takes his first shot for record. It is a seven at one o'clock. He marks it with a dot, which he labels "D." He does not move his sights off a single shot.

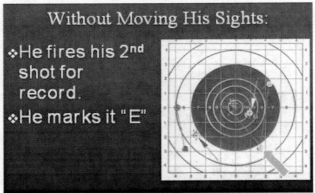

Fig. 170

He fires again. His second shot for record is a six, just out of the black at five o'clock. He marks it with a dot and labels it "E." **Again, without moving the sights, he fires his third shot.**

160

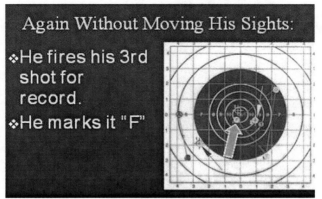

Fig. 171

It is an X at seven o'clock. It is marked with a dot and labeled "F."

He draws a light line from each dot to form a triangle.

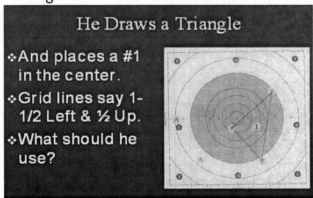

Fig. 172

A number one with a small circle around it is placed in the center of this triangle. **He is <u>now</u> ready to move his sights**. His last shot was an X, but he knows he needs a sight change. All three shots <u>could</u> be right next to each other, making a small triangle. The principle is the same. He moves his sights now, not after five or six shots. Move sights neither too soon nor too late.

Fig. 173

From the center of the triangle, 1/2 or 3/4 of a minute left would be good. I'll use 1/2. 1/4 of a minute up is the elevation change. From 2+, come left 1/2 and 1/4 minute up. The new cone center is located just in the X ring at eleven o'clock.

> He takes another 3 shot group.
> He marks the 2nd triangle "2"
> Smaller and fewer sight
> adjustments result.
> Zero is "Centered" faster.

Fig. 174

The shooter takes another three shot group and checks the center of it to see if a sight adjustment is needed. **By making smaller and fewer sight adjustments, our Marksman has centered his group faster and far more accurately than the "Let's chase the spotter" method.**

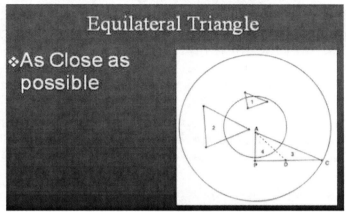

Fig. 175

When you fire your three shot group and form the triangle, there are several things to keep in mind. If all three shots are fairly close together, as in triangle number one (See Figure 175). The shots should be within, or close to, your inner cone.

Triangle number two is larger. The shots are spread wider within the cone. **The two triangles have one important point in common; the sides are fairly close to being the same**. The center of triangle number one is just inside the inner cone. The center of triangle number two is just outside the inner cone. In either case, as long as the sides are near the same length, then it is all right to move the sights (based on the center of the triangle and the amended rule).

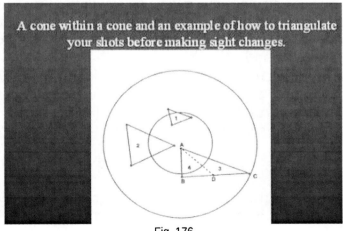

Fig. 176

163

There is one more important point to cover. **Adjusting for the "standard deviation"**: The wide shot you called good. In Figure 176, with the third triangle, if you had fired shots A, B and C, consider the two close shots, A and B, as being in or near the inner cone, and shot C, as part of the standard deviation.

The number three is the center of that triangle. **You need to "adjust for" the standard deviation** by placing a dot along the line B-C at a point about the same distance as A-B. Mark it D, forming a new, smaller triangle. I've labeled it number four. Now you can make your sight adjustment.

IF YOU HAVE A BAD CALL

Remember, the amended rule and the cone is good only if you do all the things required, i.e., sight alignment, trigger control, etc. If you have a bad call or muscle the rifle, THAT shot cannot be included in plotting the triangle. You have to disregard that shot when plotting. You will, of course, still be scored for the bad shot. Just don't plot it for the purpose of moving the sights.

This chapter has dealt with the method I recommend for new shooters and any shooter having trouble centering his groups. I use this method when I'm coaching someone in that area of experience. Do I use this method for myself? NO!! I DO use the amended rule. I am aware of my cone. I do know that when I move my sights I'm moving the center of my cone, not just an individual shot. I will, however, move off a single shot if I'm sure it was a good call.

I trust my rifle, ammunition, equipment, and my own ability enough to assume the shot was within or near my inner cone. A High Master cannot afford two shots in the same place, if they are out of the ten ring. The competition is fierce.

ZERO SHIFTS

I have a problem that I'm sure other people are experiencing. As I am shooting, at one point in my string of Slow Fire, my zero will shift.

I don't know if the rifle has heated up, if the bedding has shifted, if the sights moved, or what causes it. The zero will shift anywhere from 1/2 to 3/4, even up to 1 1/2 minutes.

One day I was testing a hand load. I had the rifle benched at 100 yards, with a 24-power scope. The first seven or eight rounds were grouping nicely in the left side of a 3/4" black paster. The next shot jumped about 1/2 minute to the right. I did not move the sights just to see what would happen. The rifle started to group again just in and out of the paster on the right side.

A zero shift at 100 yards is bad enough, but having one at 600 yards can hurt your score. When it happens, you have to make an instant decision. Did I call the shot correctly? Was the shot a wide one and part of the standard deviation? **Did I have a "zero shift?"**

If you had a zero shift, and you do nothing, the next shot could also be out in the same spot. If the shot was a wide one and part of the standard deviation and you take a full movement on the sights, you may be out the other side with your next shot.

If I should have a wide nine at six o'clock and I had a good call, I would use caution. I do not want another one in the same spot nor do I want a nine out the top. I would come up a quarter of a minute; maybe 3/8ths. <u>If I did have a zero shift, this would put me back into the ten ring. Granted, it would be low in the ten ring, but better than a nine.</u>

If there weren't a zero shift, the quarter or 3/8ths up would not be enough to put me out the top. I would get shots high in the ten ring and know the bad one was just a wide one. I would gradually work my way back down into the X-ring.

Common problems with the rifle that can cause large groups

If the chamber and/or the barrel is dirty the size of your cone will be larger than it should be. After it is cleaned your Cone (Group Size) will be smaller. This is particularly true if the rifle has some mechanical problem, See Fig. 177.

After the problem is corrected, once again your Cone (Group Size) will be smaller. Fig. 177 applies to basically all rifles.

COMMON RIFLE PROBLEMS
that can cause Large Groups

1. The chamber is dirty
2. The barrel is dirty
3. The barrel is shot out.
4. Throat erosion.
5. Incorrect headspace.
6. The bedding is loose.
7. The barrel is incorrectly fitted.
8. The trigger is worn.
9. The sights are loose.
10. The sight base is loose.
11. A bad firing pin main spring.
12. The sights are not tracking—backlash.

Fig. 177

Fig. 177 applies to basically all rifles AND **Fig. 178 can ALSO apply to the M-14 (M1A).**

MATCH SERVICE RIFLE
- Other problems that can occur

1. The hand guard may be loose.
2. The gas plug may be loose.
3. The gas piston may be sticking.
4. There could be binding between the stock ferrule & the lower band.
5. Lack of lubrication.
6. Crack in the stock.
7. Loose flash suppressor.
8. Misaligned flash suppressor.

Fig. 178

Well, there you are. Chapters 7, 8 and 9 are what I call "The Advanced Theory." I have had hundreds of people tell me "Thank you, that has helped my shooting tremendously." I have also had 3 or 4 people tell me "You are full of "S--T, it does not work."

I am not telling anyone they have to use it, but "Try it, you may like it."

IN CONCLUSION

I hope you have enjoyed reading this as much as I enjoyed writing it. The only major point to cover about the cone is how to reduce the size of the cone (your groups).

I do have a suggestion for you. During the shooting season, take down this book about every three months and read it again. You will be amazed at how much you will learn the second and third time. There is so much information you may not grasp it all the first time through.

If you read it several times and <u>apply</u> what you have learned, your scores <u>will</u> improve. Help the Juniors and the new shooters, they are the future of the sport. The things we do to help others is small payment for the good things in our lives.

One last thing...

If there is anything you do not understand and you would like some help, please feel free to call me at 334-347-0020, I can talk faster than I can type.

Keep reading for the next chapter on "Analyzing Groups."

CHAPTER TEN

Fig. 179

The following pictures are **samples of rapid fire groups**, what causes them and how to correct them.

By looking at your own or someone else's <u>rapid fire groups</u>, you can determine what is the problem and possibly how to correct that problem.

The 1st group shown (Fig. 180) the shots are strung out from the center of the black down towards 5 o'clock.

Prone position
some of the possible causes are:

a. Failure to get left elbow under the rifle
b. Sling Slipping
c. Jerking the Trigger

Fig. 180

Corrections:

a.   Left elbow should be under the Rifle (That may not always be possible, due to the magazine on the AR-15 or the M1A) at least try to get the left arm parallel to the rifle.

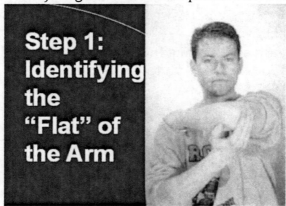

Fig. 181

b. "Flat of the arm" above the elbow touches mat, not the elbow (Bend your left arm toward you and touch you right shoulder with your left hand see Fig. 181. Raise your arm parallel to the ground, now touch your left elbow with the fingers of your right hand. Move your fingers of your right hand slowly down and toward your left shoulder. Move your finger tips down and around the curve of the elbow. You will feel a large flat area about your elbow. **That flat area is where the arm should touch the shooting mat, NOT the sharply bent elbow**. As you are going down into position for the prone position, extend your left shoulder towards the target, which will help to get the "Flat of the Arm" onto the shooting mat. See Fig. 188 to see the results of shooting on a sharply bent elbow. Your shots will be strung out from left to right.)

c. Adjustable hand stop (on a Match Rifle)

d. Sling cuff – does not slip – (on a Match Rifle)

e. Service rifle sling – 1 ¼" wide, good keepers and they should be tight

f. Take up slack & squeeze trigger as if in slow fire

Sitting:
some of the possible causes are:

a. Possible sling slipping

b. More likely left elbow slipping down inside left knee

Corrections:

a. Try crossed ankle Position or the figure 4 position (The figure four position is similar to the crossed ankle position. The right leg is drawn back a little until the ankle and the instep of the right foot is under and supports the calf of the left leg.)

b. Use some Adhesive spray like Hawkeye

c. Shooting pants have pads on the legs to match up with the pads on the shooting jacket

The next group is Center to 11 O'clock

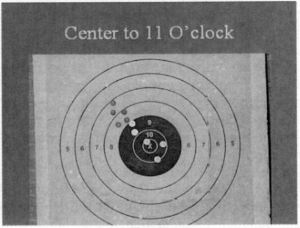

Fig. 182

Problem:

a. Not following through
b. Anticipating recoil
c. Pulls rifle to rear, lowers shoulder to right & raises muz-zle to left

Corrections:

a. Good stock weld (Your cheek is **Firmly** placed on the stock of the rifle)
b. Let head ride with recoil
c. Wait for rifle to push shoulder & *move* with it
d. _**Concentration:**_ should be centered on sight alignment & trigger control!
e. Ignore recoil

Shots Scattered, No Particular Pattern (Large)

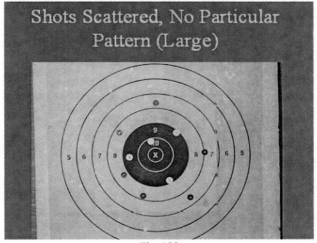

Fig. 183

Problem:

a. **Poor trigger control**

Correction:

a. Practice trigger control exercise (See Chapter Four)
b. Finger on "Autopilot" (Finger comes off the trigger when you feel the rifle move)

Good Group, Upper Right

Fig. 184

Problem:

a. Failure to properly adjust sights (Windage & Elevation)
b. 2nd group may be centered
c. But, you Lost a lot of points on 1st string

Corrections:

a. Make sure your zero is on before firing 1st group
(Dummy)

Good Group Out at Six O'clock

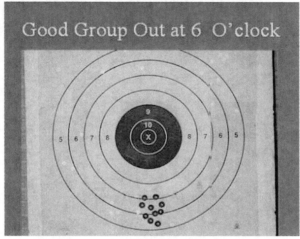

Fig. 185

Problem:

a. Forgot to put your elevation on
b. Had it on & counted down & did not put it back on

Corrections:

a. Keep your head where it can get some sunshine.

Good Group Out at Twelve O'clock

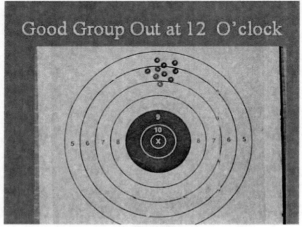

Fig. 186

Problem:

a. Put your elevation on twice
b. Double doped (Put your Elevation on TWICE)

Correction:

a. Again, Keep your head where it can get some sunshine.

Good Group Out at Three or Nine O'clock

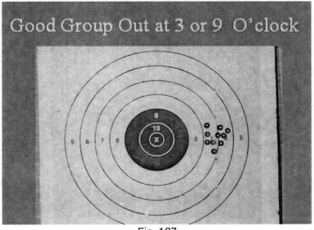

Fig. 187

Problem:

a. Windage knob was a full turn off

Correction:

a. One more time, Keep your head where it can get some sunshine.

Center to Seven O'clock

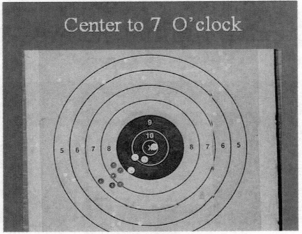

Fig. 188

Problem:

a. Anticipating recoil
b. "Bucking"
c. "Flinching"
d. Shoving your shoulder into it

Corrections:

a. Simply let the recoil happen
b. Concentration centered on sight alignment & trigger squeeze
c. Finger should come off the trigger automatically if you feel like you are flinching.

Shots Well Placed Vertically but Strung Out Horizontally

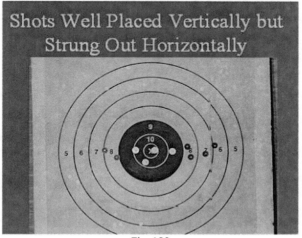

Fig. 189

Problem:

1. Canting the sights (The sights are tilted off to one side)
>   a. Sling too tight
>>   Impossible to get sights vertical
>   b. Hard to get left elbow under rifle
2. Increase cant as muscles tire
3. Too high of a position, rifle propped up on a sharply bent elbow (See previously mentioned "Flat of the Arm.")

Corrections:

a. Get left hand well forward
b. Forearm nearly touching the mat (Caution; it is not legal to shoot with the forearm <u>touching</u> the mat)
c. Flat of the arm ***above*** the elbow touches the mat, not the elbow

Shots Well Placed Horizontally but Strung Up & Down

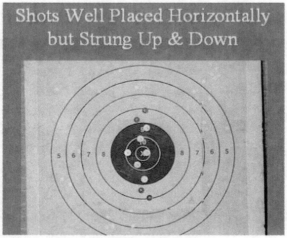

Fig. 190

Problem:

a. <u>**Improper breathing (Most common problem) See Chapter One**</u>
b. Crawling

Corrections:

1. A breath should be taken prior to each shot
    a. Inhaling lowers front sight
    b. Exhaling raises front sight
2. A breath taken in & let out until the same "Lung Pressure" is felt
3. Consistency
    a. Most important
    b. Do a task exactly the same each & every time
4. Crawling
    a. Position on ground not solid
    b. Tend to slide backwards after each shot
        I. Must correct after each shot

c. Two or three shots without correcting, causing the higher hits

    I. Lower hits coming after you correct

d. Use adhesive spray on both elbows

    I. Have toes dug in

    II. Have body well behind the rifle

Center to Six O'clock

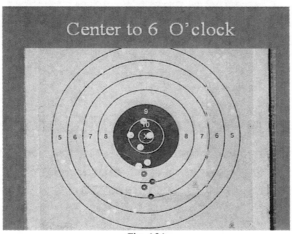

Fig. 191

1. Sling is slipping
2. Left hand is slipping forward on the stock
3. Slipping back and crawling forward too far
4. Good indication left elbow is under rifle because the shots are not strung out left to right

Center to Nine O'clock

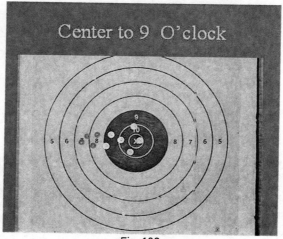

Fig. 192

Dragging Wood (See Chapter Four)

a. Allowing trigger finger to lay too tightly against the stock
b. Having trigger finger placed improperly
c. Pushing trigger to the side, taking front sight with it

Shots Scattered,
No Particular Pattern (Close)

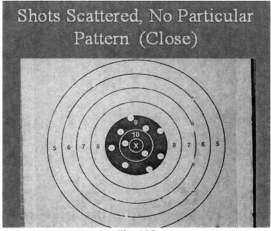

Shots Scattered, No Particular
Pattern (Close)

Fig. 193

Improper Focus (See Chapter Two)

1. Focus on front sight ___not___ the bullseye
2. With proper focus 9's become 10's

I was shooting a match at Twenty Nine Palms, Marine Corps base. Twenty shoots Off-Hand (Standing) at 200 yards. My 1st ten shots were all in the black, but I only had two ten's and eight nines. I realized I had been focusing on the target and not on the front sight. I gave myself a "Mental Dropkick" and for the second ten shots I focused on the front sight. This time I had eight ten's and X's and just two nines.

My First 10 shots Off Hand - I was focusing on *the Bullseye*

Fig. 194

My Second 10 shots Off Hand - After using the Proper Focus

Fig. 195

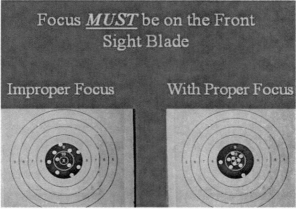

Fig. 196

Focus *MUST* be on the Front Sight Blade.

APPENDIX A

Some of the most common mechanical problems causing large groups:
1. The chamber is dirty
2. The barrel is dirty
3. The barrel is shot out
4. Throat erosion
5. The crown is damaged
6. Incorrect headspace
7. The bedding is loose
8. The barrel is incorrectly fitted
9. The trigger is wearing
10. The sights are loose
11. The sight base is loose
12. A bad firing pin main spring
13. Sights not tracking - backlash

In addition to the items listed above, the Service Match Rifle could have the following problems:

1. The hand guard may be loose
2. The gas plug may be loose
3. The gas piston may be sticking
4. There could be binding between the stock ferrule and the lower band
5. Lack of lubrication
6. Crack in the stock
7. Loose flash suppressor.
8. Misaligned flash suppressor.

APPENDIX B

The following is a list (in alphabetical order) of friends and shooting buddies in the state of Wisconsin. They provide shooting related goods and services. They all have been very helpful tome and this is my way of saying **"Thanks."**

Jack Krieger

People are always asking me "who has the better rifle barrel, Jack Krieger or Boots Obermeyer? I have both and I can't tell the difference and neither can you. They are both excellent!!! Jack offers fitting services for his barrels. He designed and built two forearm systems for "floating the barrel in the AR-15s.

KRIEGER BARRELS, INC.
2024 Mayfield Rd.
Richfield, WI 53076
262-628-8558
www.kriegerbarrels.com

Boots Obermeyer

I'm a shooting junkie and Boots is my pusher. Boots has thirty five years experience as a barrel maker and for a one man operation, he produces more barrels than some of the larger companies. Both Boots and I have shot scores of 100 with ten Xs using his barrels. He usually has barrels in stock. Boots carries shooting equipment and reloading components at a small mark up.

OBERMEYER RIFLED BARRELS
23122 60th Street
Bristol, WI. 53104-9734
262-843-3537
obermeyerbarrels.com

Northern Competition
Lee Penzkowski has lost his battle with cancer.
Rest in peace, Lee

APPENDIX C

200 YARD OFF HAND AND RAPID FIRE SITTING

300 yard target with the "Amended Minute of Angle" grid lines

1000 yard target with the "Amended Minute of Angle" grid lines

191

APPENDIX D

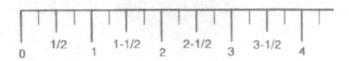

THE GAUGE

Copy or trace this gauge to make your own.

ATTENTION!

The gauge shown above is drawn according to the **AMENDED RULE** and will help to explain the text and the sight adjustments you should make.

This ruler (gauge) is not to scale (as the print/ebook image size may change depending on your readers screen size etc.). If you want to make one to scale for your scorebook, follow the instructions in the text.

Shooting Products
from Jim Owens

Sight Alignment, Trigger Control & The Big Lie
A Power-packed book that has helped many shooters improve their groups and scores, some by as much as forty or fifty points. This book covers not only the basics of breathing, natural point of aim, sight alignment, sight picture, focus and trigger control exercises. It has sections on Mental conditioning, marking the sights, zeroing, normal come ups, light effects, damage to the crown, care in cleaning, throat erosion and bullet run out. There is also an advanced theory that has been praised by High Masters and Marksmen.

New CD version includes a new chapter **"Analyzing Groups"** with more and better pictures for the price of the book. Yes, you may print off pages as you need them for the range!
 $14.95 plus $2.80 S&H

Mastering the Leather Sling and Shooting Positions
Learn to assemble the leather sling in the same method taught by the Marine Corps Team. Follow a four-step program to shooting positions, the likes of which you have never seen before. As an added bonus, receive a five-step theory that could increase your off-hand three to ten points.

Now on CD, with a new chapter on the **No-Pulse Sling**, with more and better pictures for the price of the book. Yes, you may print off pages as you need them for the range!
 $12.95 plus $2.80 S&H

Care, Cleaning and Sportsmanship
The Care and Cleaning of Rifles, with particular attention to the Service Rifles. Tips on Bullet Seating, An interview, Questions & Answers with Boots Obermeyer, Jack Krieger, Charlie Milazzo and Mike Bykowski. Also, Interviews with Seven National Champions as how they clean their bores. An extensive chapter on "Moly Coating." The positive side of Sportsmanship.
 $12.95 plus $2.80 S&H

"FOUR BOOK SET"

Get all four books at a special reduced rate! *Save $5.85*
"Reading the Wind and Coaching Techniques", "Sight Alignment, Trigger Control and the Big Lie", "Leather Sling and Shooting Positions", "Care, Cleaning and Sportsmanship"

All four together on CD, with all the added chapters and wind charts from each individual book as well as all the newer and better pictures!
$43.95 plus $5.40 S&H

Advance Theory CD

For many years shooters have made a sight adjustment and have come out the other side. Someone would tell them, "you must put one click on the rifle and one click in your head". The "Windage and Elevation" rule states, "One click will move the strike of the bullet one inch per 100 yards. Jim's Advance Theory says, You must do two things with it: (1) Memorize it, because people will talk about it, and (2) Forget it, it does not work!
Jim gives you an alternate theory in three Power Point Presentations on the CD - That Does Work!
And, get Personal Support after viewing the CD! If you have any questions or do not understand something, just call Jim at 334-347-0020 and he will be more than happy to help you.
$20 plus $2.20 S&H

Reading The Wind 2 CD Set

The first CD has Jim's "*Reading the Wind*" that he uses in his classes; the most recent and best efforts.
Included:

- Different forces affecting the bullet
- A simple system anyone can use to "Read The Wind"
- Simple and inexpensive aides to help you
- A detailed description as to reading the mirage
- A simple and the most accurate way to read flags
- "Alternative" methods when the mirage or flags are not readable

The second CD has 22 Sets of really good Wind Charts - PLUS a bonus short class on using Kentucky Windage.
$25 plus $3.50 S&H

Line & Pit Procedures CD

When we 1st participate in a new sport we are a little intimidated. We don't know what to expect. We do not want to make a mistake, look foolish, maybe having someone yell at us or mess someone else up.

Well, come along with me. We are going to a High Power Rifle Match. We are going from start to finish. From the time we arrive at the Range, to checking in at the stat office, getting assigned our relay, dropping our gear off at the ready line and reporting to the Pits. •We are going to be there all day. We will see the different relays fire the Match and in turn see the different problems that can come up and how they are handled. •We are going to find out where to go and when. We will find out what we have to do when we get there and what supplies we will need. We will find out the proper way to run a target, both in slow fire and rapid fire. How to handle the different situations. •We will learn the Range Commands, both Line and The Pits. We will learn the flow of the Match.

I am going to show you some of the small tricks I have learned in over 45 years of shooting. **$11.95 plus $2.20 S&H**

Score Keeping CD

You learn by doing! After the instruction phase you actually score a shooter in both slow fire and rapid fire. The different problems that can occur will be presented as you score the shooter. You will get years of experience in a single setting. In fact, you will know more than most people that have been shooting 5 to 10 years.
 $11.95 plus $2.20 S&H

The Complete AR-15 High Performance Guide

The latest on accuracy modifications and accessories for "Space Guns" and Service Rifles. It features an extensive hand loading section and shooting techniques specifically suited to the AR-15. It also includes special chapters with 11-time Champion G. David Tubb on the AR-10/SR-25; USAMU head C.I. Boyd and ace shooter Sgt. Lew Tippie; gunsmith Derrick Martin; and the input of a dozen other industry leaders! Written by a High Master Service Rifle Shooter, critics have said it is one of the finest books they've ever read on the subject of High Power Rifle Competition.
 $28.95 plus $5.40 S&H

Hand loading for Competition
A brand new book by the author and publisher of The Competitive AR15. It's a guide to "practical precision" in producing high-performance ammunition.
$ 34.95 plus $5.40 S&H

Jim Owens Data Book
Some of the features are Eight Sets of Wind Charts, A Wind Speed Estimating Guide, More than Twice the # of pages., Larger plotting areas, All Scoring rings are Proportional, Jim Owens "Amended" grid lines, Twin plotting bulls for rapid fire, A "Gun Round Count" page, A Check list for items to bring to the range, A chart detailing the scores needed for each classification, A chart giving the dimensions of the scoring rings, A chart describing the scoring system, A guide for normal come-ups from 100 to 1,000 yards in 100 yard increments, A chart explaining the "9-Yes, 9-No" problems. This data book is more than a $60.00 value.
$15.95 Plus $5.40 S&H. Sent via Priority Mail

NEW - *Use of the Jim Owens Data Books*
$15.00 plus S&H or $10.00 plus S&H if ordered with any data book!

Jim Owens (Long Range) Data Book
Some of the features are: 54 two sided pages for the 600 yard stage and 54 two sided pages for the 800/900/1,000 yard target, 14 Sets of Wind Charts, A Wind Speed Estimating Guide, Larger plotting areas, All Scoring rings are Proportional, Jim Owens "Amended" grid lines, A "Gun Round Count" page, A chart detailing the scores needed for each classification, A chart giving the dimensions of the scoring rings, A chart describing the scoring system, A guide for normal come-ups from 100 to 1,000 yards in 100 yard increments.
$15.95 Plus $5.40 S&H. Sent via Priority Mail

Contact me at:

Jim Owens
112 Red Wing Dr.
Enterprise, AL 36330
334-347-0020
Top@JarHeadTop.com
www.JarHeadTop.com

What they are saying about
Sight Alignment, Trigger Control & The Big Lie

"My scores have improved drastically. I thank you for your books. High Power shooting is enjoyable when you do better."
   —Neal Trubitt

"After shooting my first match a few weeks ago. One of the guys from my club loaned me a set of your books. I can not thank you enough. I can understand what you are talking about. I know the next match will go much better for me. Thanks Again"
   —John DeMoss

"Your series of books and tapes have helped me make the first daunting steps and I entered my first competitive event ever, the 2004 NRA High Power Week Competition at Camp Perry. Your Data Book is the best that I have seen and all the information that you had put together and your personal commitment to Juniors in the sport is indeed commendable."
   —Steven Field

"Your books were so great and helpful, I gave them to my Dad, and have not seen them back! So I need another set!"
   —Another happy customer

CPSIA information can be obtained
at www.ICGtesting.com
Printed in the USA
LVOW07s0726021017
550632LV00001B/10/P